TRUST IN YOUR CHILD

Trust in Your Child - A parent's Guide to raising
resilient and happy children

© EmpowerMind Books 2017

Writers: Mitzi & Jørgen Svenstrup
Editor: Anne Albrecht
Graphic design & illustration: Meta Emilie Hansen
Translation: Sinéad Quirke

Print and distribution by IngramSpark - Lightning
Source 2017

ISBN: 978-87-993939-8-5

Mitzi & Jørgen Svenstrup

TRUST
IN YOUR CHILD

**A parental guide to raising
resilient and happy children**

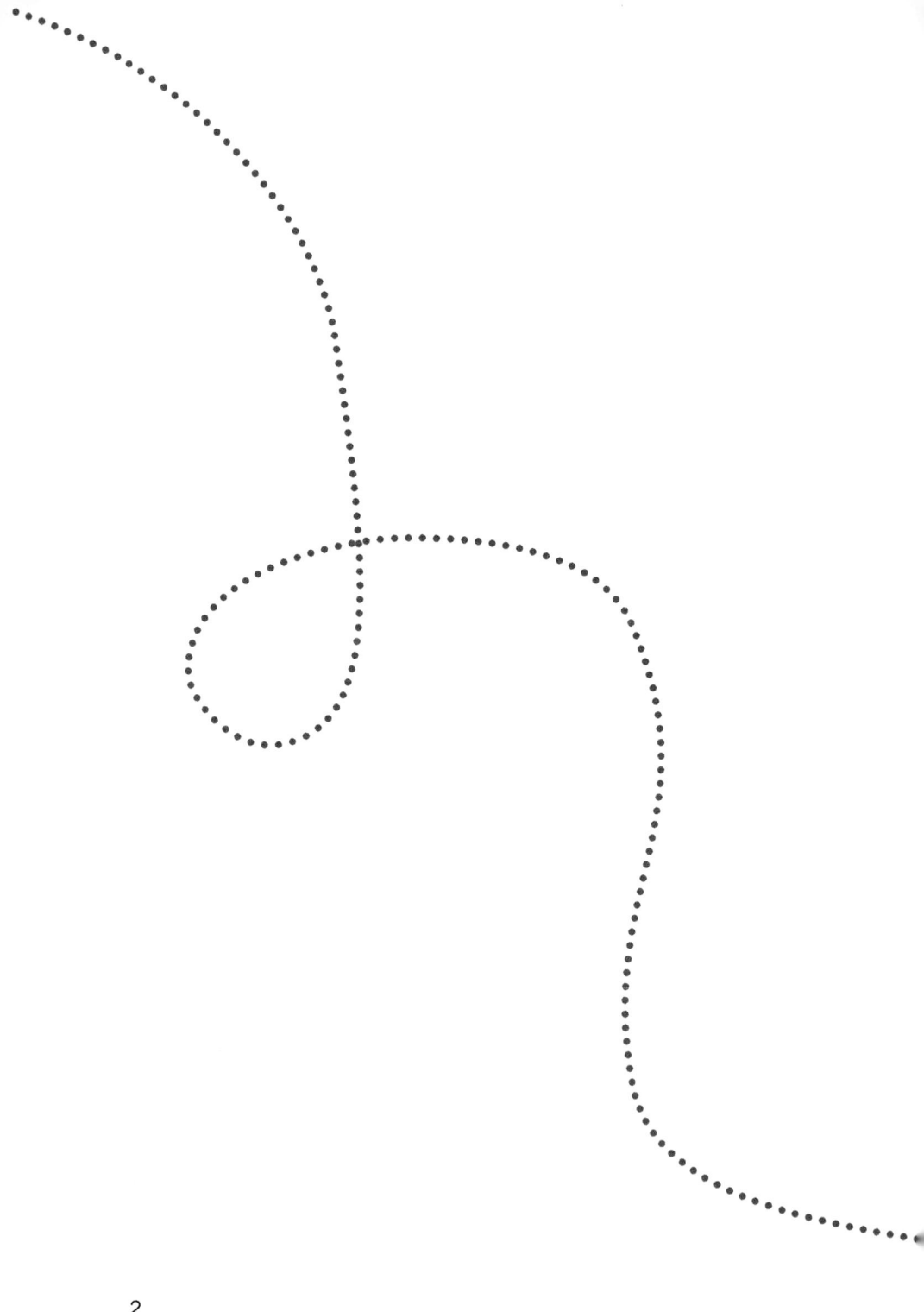

2

For Amelina

You make us so happy, because you are you!

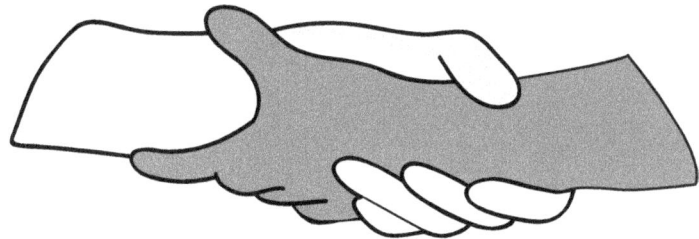

Contents

HABITS
OF THE
HEART

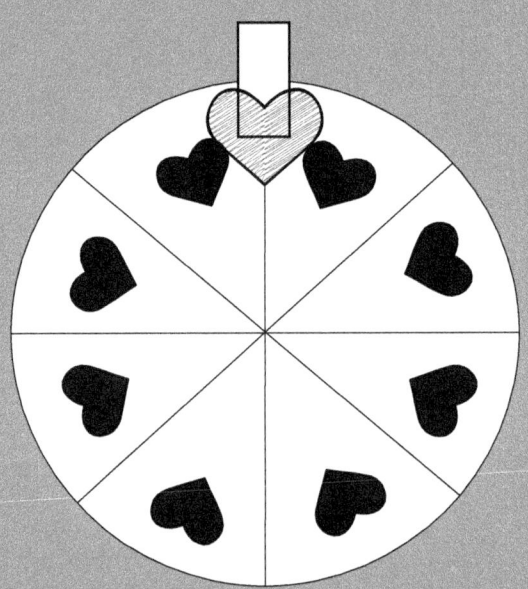

Foreword by Charlotte Guldberg,
chairperson, the National Council for Children, Denmark

Children are the family's biggest reason to smile, so how hard can it be? As parents, we repeatedly ask both ourselves and others this question, especially when it comes to ensuring a achievable and dynamic existence for our children amidst the busy everyday landscape. What psychological and practical provisions do we need to make in order to experience and perceive parenthood as a golden investment opportunity? That is what the chapters in this book are all about.

Parenting is, naturally, diversely rooted in practical application, negotiation and the reconciliation of the balance of power. Above all, it's about emotional relationships and connections, where attachment-style, personal history, reciprocity and confidentiality are of great importance. How can we create balance between these aspects, when we're also responsible for managing our child's well-being and development?

One thing is certain: if we allow ourselves to be positively affected by the sometimes complex interaction process of parenthood, then there is a wonderful added benefit waiting for us. Obviously, this can be extremely challenging for the modern family. It requires adjusting expectations – and being a parent is a huge turning point in anyone's life. To include a little person in the framework of adult relationships can be complicated enough for many people, as each person's motives are always present and wrestling to come out on top. Communication flows between family members, duties and responsibilities are persistently present, and should be consistent; attitudes and values need to be tested; interpretations thrown around; and intentions discussed – and all while the unexpected awaits.

You can almost be tempted into thinking that parenting is not for beginners.

Fortunately, this is not the case. This book illustrates that life, as a couple or as a family, is easier and more enjoyable if we practise both our ability to be influenced by the child and our capacity to accept the child's right to influence. As an old Indian proverb says, it is about trying to "walk a mile in the other's moccasins".

This book is about walking hand-in-hand with your child, letting the child feel that "I, your parent, am with you, and I appreciate that you are who you are." It is brimming with instructions on how and why it is important to come together with your child on this journey.

The authors focus positively on immersive understanding, which is obtained through respect for the child's situation. He recommends that we, as adults, make the effort to think about being in the child's situation, a different landscape from the one that exists within us adults. For adults, the desire to become familiar with the child's landscape comes through exploring their paths and stories; by spending time together, by showing interest in the child's initiatives and by following up on them in our actions. This is a particularly good idea in relation to preventing recurrent conflicts and breakdowns.

Empathy, sensing the other, and the idea of physical presence seem to be some of the driving forces behind creating a shortcut to having happy children.

Jørgen Svenstrup leads the way in development-supporting options, which can always be found through the reflective handling of our own and our children's feelings and reactions. With knowledge of our feelings, we increase the possibility of interacting with the child from the child's own perspective and not only from the adult's interpretation of the child's perspective. That is a significant difference.

In other words: take your child seriously. Trust in your child.

New knowledge from the areas of organisation and management transfer elegantly to parenthood. We receive instructions for how we, as parents, can enrich everyday life in new ways, including anticipating communication traps. At the same time, the book offers tools designed to help us create an appreciative and loving environment that can help us keep track of and regulate the heavily invested emotions in our family circles.

Through mutual inclusion, cohesion and participation in the child's beliefs, their feelings and common sense can grow hand-in-hand with ours throughout their childhood. The positive consequences are obvious, and one of life's greatest mysteries – a whole new world opens up to us when we become parents – becomes' a gift to be presented, thanks to the author's views of how parenting can be strengthened.

The everyday stresses of a busy lifestyle can make us blind to ensuring that our children receive the best we have to offer: we should practice our capacity to love every day. Thankfully, the book also provides instructions for this.

Do giving and receiving love follow naturally from each other? It is indisputably a strong component for a good childhood. The book is therefore primarily about what I would call habits of the heart; actions which ensure a dignified existence and have an influence on our own life, day after day.

Children carry their experiences with them into adulthood, and through interaction with other people, they train themselves in being understood in social relationships, interpreting, understanding and respecting their own and others' feelings and choices of behaviour. Emotional and social competences can be practised. This happens every day in the family. This book provides awareness training in empathy and decision making, and immediately opens up the opportunity to give children a greater self-awareness and understanding of how emotions affect themselves and others. Through the democratic participation process, the child learns to take responsibility and contribute constructively to the community both inside and outside the family.

The authors share, willingly and openly, from their own experiences as parents by highlighting key areas of children's lives. They touch upon the deep existential questions and introduce possibilities that can help strengthen parenting.

Children are all different and have different needs, resources and preferences. That is within their full right. This is emphasised again and again in this book. Therefore, this particular book's positive thinking, parenting strategies and practical instructions are highly recommended.

Children accept with open hearts.

Charlotte Guldberg,
Chairperson,
The National Council for Children, Denmark.

A CHANGE FOR LIFE

Brainwash your child – Why not? You do it anyway!

You need a driving licence to drive a car, a hunting licence to hunt and a dog licence to have a dog. But you don't actually need any qualifications or certificates to have children, other than your concept of and assumptions about parenthood. Fortunately, the majority of us have some idea of what it takes to make a good daily life for our children.

Yet often, our feelings and unconscious choices prevent us from doing the very best for our children. We can be so stressed that we are constantly ready to fly off the handle. We are so caught up in day-to-day chores – packed lunches, play dates, homework and treating head lice – that we are too busy to be present in the moment; we don't reflect on what we are doing. We forget to involve our children, to give them ownership of their own lives, and to listen to their versions of the world. And above all, unwittingly, though with the best of intentions, we brainwash our children in the most inappropriate way.

Our children mean everything to us, but without realising it, we thwart their optimal well-being. We want to eradicate this. Therefore, this book is the presentation of our philosophy - *EmpowerMind Training*. *EmpowerMind Training* can, with a little effort, bring about a big change for your child – now and for the rest of their life.

WE DO THE BEST WE CAN

As the authors of this book, we firmly believe that every parent around the world does the very best they can to help their children get a good start in life. We believe that this also applies to you. This is the premise of *Trust in your Child*.

Moreover, we believe that we can continue to improve our parenting skills – without it taking more time, emitting more CO_2 or costing a penny. We are convinced that we as parents, and with relatively little effort, can make a big difference in how we act with our children. All it requires of us is to take notice of what we actually do and say to them.

> **As soon as you start your journey with this book, you will see yourself, your child and your family in a new light.** ,,

As parents, we have no desire to feel guilty, particularly not for something we should or should not have done. We look forward to and seek possibilities in parenting. Let yourself be inspired by the advice in this book and take from it what you feel is most useful to you.

Once you become aware of all the assumptions and beliefs you have about your children and your family, you will also become aware of the opportunities for reducing conflicts over issues such as doing homework, going to bed and eating vegetables. In short, 'witching hours' will be replaced by seeing eye-to-eye with your child, allowing you to give your child the best opportunities to succeed in the complex world that awaits them.

As soon as you start your journey with this book, you will see yourself, your child and your family in a new light. Or it can just decorate your bedside table...

IT'S JUST NOT GOOD ENOUGH – THAT'S WHY WE WROTE THIS BOOK

The idea for *Trust in your Child* came to us through our personal development work with adults, for which we developed – and continue to use – a new technique, based on the latest neuro-research and a mix of coaching, positive psychology, mental training, neuro-linguistic programming (NLP) and hypnosis.

This technique is called *EmpowerMind Training*. It's a potent mix that influences both the conscious and unconscious mind. These principles, combined with our experiences and research in this field, form the mind-set of this book.

We are the founders and owners of *EmpowerMind Denmark*, which offers coaching courses with an internationally-recognised coaching certificate (International Association of Coaching Institutes, ICI) and involves coaching and *minding* for leaders, managers, employees and individuals who want to develop professionally and/or personally. We have worked with leaders for over 20 years and have a particular focus on long-term developmental processes.

AN UNEXPECTED BONUS

In coaching or *EmpowerMind training*, it's rare for participants to acquire new knowledge and tools only for use in their work-life, especially as the process is much more about personal development, which can be exercised anywhere: at work, in parenting, in our relationships, on committees, on the football team...

Experience has shown us that participants who are also parents receive an unexpected bonus, an eye-opener: they realise that by making small changes to and in their children's upbringing, they can bring about real change in both the short- and long-run. Not so much by coaching or *minding* their children directly, but by adjusting their 'control' over their children and making a minor change in their behaviour towards them.

This book is obviously not the definitive truth; rather, it is a way for us to share our knowledge and experiences of what works for people in a developmental process. If you increase your awareness of how you interact with your child in everyday life, we think you will find that the rest will follow automatically.

Our philosophy is that we must engage our children instead of just educating them. We believe that children are independent, thinking and feeling individuals. They are not just mini copies of ourselves that we must raise in our image and according to our unconscious will.

We must *engage* our children instead of just educating them.

We are very inspired by the concept of child-involvement rather than the more traditional concepts of child-rearing. What's unique to this book is that we have adapted the most current principles within neuro-research, leadership and personal development, so that they can be used in relation to your child.

It works for Mitzi, Amelina and I – imagine if it worked for you and your child!

A WONDERFUL CHILD?

You will read many everyday stories about children and adults in the book. One person you will meet consistently is Amelina, our daughter. Mitzi and I will also share the occasional anecdote from our life.

Amelina is in no way intended to be a representative for all (Danish) children, as we do not believe any two children or their family conditions are exactly alike.

Instead, we use everyday examples of Amelina to show what the coaching and minding child-involvement concept can bring about, when applied as consistently as possible.

When you read the stories about Amelina, you can choose to believe it won't work with your child, or you can choose to believe that it would.

The choice is yours!

Yes, Amelina is a wonderful child. So is your child! For they are our children.

On the other hand, we are not wonderful parents. We occasionally 'have enough' and yell at our children after we have said the same thing a thousand times. And we tend to forget what is most important to us when we are facing an inbox of unanswered emails. But we constantly work to improve ourselves both as parents – and as people.

We tend to forget what is really most important to us. **"**

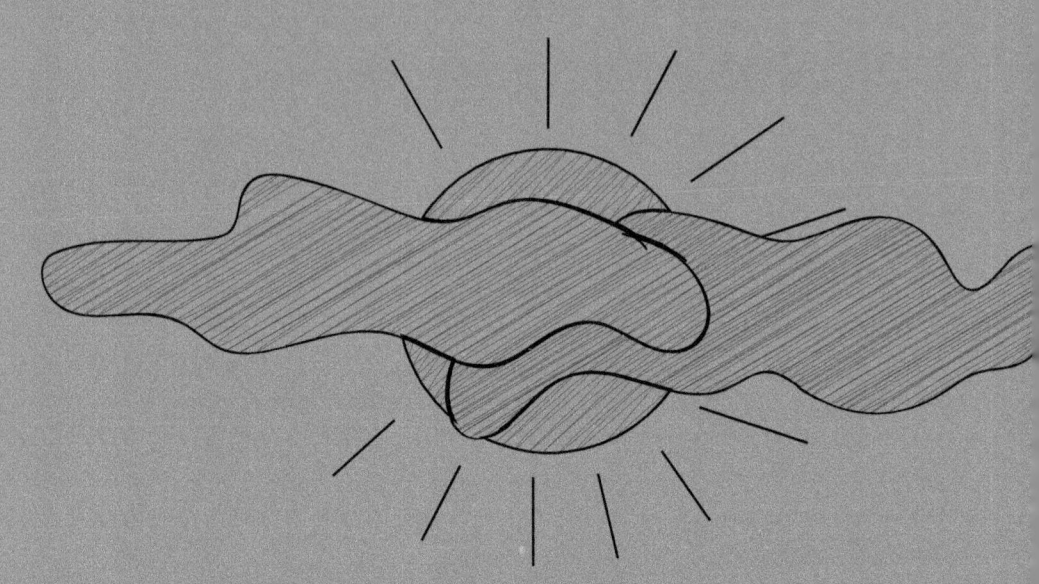

The problem with common sense and feelings is that they can cloud our judgement.

"

BREAK THE RULES!

As soon as Mitzi and I had Amelina, we embraced her and saw her as a project. That perhaps sounds quite cold and clinical, but it isn't.

Projects have always been complex tasks. We throw all our love and energy into them. That is how we see our role as parents. It is our life's greatest project and, therefore, too precious to handle carelessly.

At the same time, it is a problem for contemporary society that parents have generally begun to see their children as projects. According to experts that is the single biggest reason for our children being egocentric, spoiled and not taking others into account. This is because we, as parents, place too much focus on our wishes for our children, which leads to parents often – and with the best of intentions – removing the obstacles encountered by their children on their paths.

Experts have called us curling parents, helicopter parents or just modern parents. They are worried that children won't be able to deal with adversity because they don't get to experience it and, therefore, will not be equipped to deal with it when they inevitably face it later in life. In short, the over-protection of parents results in fragile children.

The reality is that we have become part of a project-oriented society and it is unthinkable that in the future we *won't* see our children as projects. Therefore, it is not about mourning the development of society, but about creating the best conditions for our children to do well – despite the 'project' approach of their well-meaning parents'.

Imagine if we, as parents, could do a fantastic job of our parenting project? That is why we need to take a step back from parenthood and look critically at what our role as parents – or as project leaders – contains and then replace everything and anything that does not benefit us or our children with something that does.

In other words: it's time to clean up parenthood! In this book, we offer two main tools for cleaning up parenthood – and they may be the two most important tools.

THE FIRST TOOL:
BRAINWASH YOUR CHILD

Of course, we know that the word brainwashing conjures up terrible connotations for most people, and since the first edition of this book came out in Denmark, we have met thousands of furious parents who have asked us how we could say such a thing. The only thing they have in common is that they have not yet read the book. If they had, they would know that we do it every day from the day our child is born. We brainwash our children in the most effective and manipulative way we can imagine: by stating and repeating an incredibly high number of assumptions and beliefs in our role as the greatest authority in the child's life – as the child's parent!

And therefore, we must warn you. From the time you read this book, you will – perhaps forever – pay more attention to what you say to your child. It is through your subconscious brainwashing that they are who they are – for better or for worse.

Here, perhaps, lies part of the reason that Danes have been named the world's happiest people for several years. What if we, in Denmark, have become better, in recent years, at brainwashing our children? Our issue is that seeing as we do it anyway, we might as well do it properly. We're looking forward to sharing this with you in the first part of the book.

THE SECOND TOOL:
LET THE CHILD BE THE EXPERT

As parents, we can and still do benefit from common sense and feelings. Most children do quite well in spite of all the obstacles unwittingly put in front of them by parents, family, friends, teachers and educators. And there is no doubt that these obstacles come with the very best of intentions.

The problem with common sense and feelings is that they can cloud our judgement.

Common sense can, to some extent, be the 'common sense of others, or reason and experience that is based, perhaps, on assumptions and beliefs that were once right, but which now are obsolete or no longer fit into our lives. Feelings are often right but even our own feelings can prevent us from doing the right thing. In this way we can – without knowing it – be the biggest obstacle to our child's well-being.

As we see it, there is only one expert here: the child.

GIVE CHILDREN A BETTER MENTAL CONDITION

In our view, a parent's primary task is to enable a child to fulfil their expert role as quickly as possible. Once the child is the expert in their own life, a high degree of freedom naturally follows, but this comes with responsibility.

That does *not* mean that we, as parents, must refrain from setting boundaries. In our view, the best thing we can do is be clear in setting boundaries for our children. It is equally important that we respect our children's boundaries. Otherwise they will not respect our or other people's boundaries. If we exceed their boundaries time and time again, we teach them that this is okay – and it is most definitely not okay in any relationship.

It is vital that we have clearly defined boundaries within which our children can freely act.

This is' no different than the current coaching and leadership philosophy, which is based on the premise that if people are to develop and become their best selves, then we must highlight the playing field with some very accurate and visible corner flags – or else just blow the whistle.

The larger the playing field, the more mental and physical force is required to keep the ball in play. So the trick is to expand the playing field in tune with the child's mental development.

A child's mental condition cannot be measured, but we can get a clear and relatively precise status-reading by moving the corner flags out slightly further than we think they can handle and seeing what happens. If the child thrives, then they are ready for something more. If the child is insecure or confused, then the corner flags need to be adjusted again. The child is not 'damaged' by this. In fact, it is much worse to have too small a playing field! We are looking forward to expanding this for you in the second part of the book.

The trick is to expand the playing field in tune with the child's mental development.

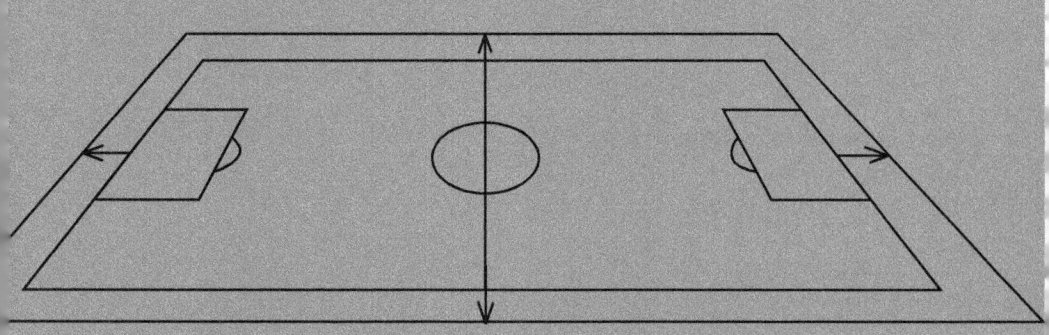

GIVE YOUR CHILD POSSIBILITIES

Marie has difficulties with maths. Emma is always slow. August gets angry easily, Albert is messy, and Josephine has always been a troublesome child...

Every day our children are exposed to limiting beliefs in the derogatory 'innocent' comments and observations that we make about them. These statements form our children's perception of themselves. Moreover, these comments are quite likely to become self-fulfilling prophecies.

In this section, we will focus on all the unconscious things that influence our children. And Mitzi and I will show you how to identify what is not constructive – and what almost certainly leads to conflict in everyday life. At the same time, we will guide you in replacing these limiting beliefs with supportive ones that will enhance your child's self-esteem.

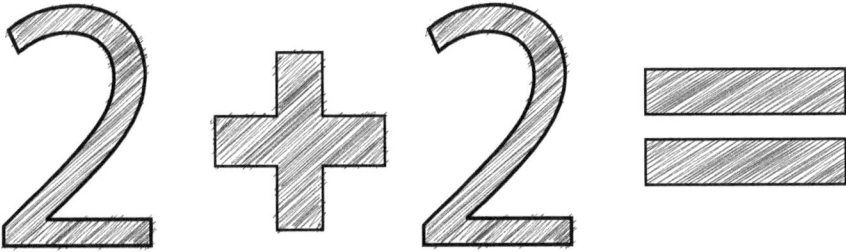

DECIDING BEFOREHAND

When Amelina was four and a half years old, we decided, with the kindergarten, that she was ready to start school after the summer holidays. This was an unusual decision, as children usually start school at age 7 in Denmark. As Amelina was four months younger than the second youngest child, she was asked to go for a three-day assessment in the current infant class, so that the teachers could assess whether or not she was ready. And as starting school is one of the big events not only in the lives of children, but also in the lives of their parents, those first three school days were, naturally, something we discussed a lot. We also discussed being careful not to raise expectations so high that it put pressure on Amelina.

The night before Amelina was to start the three-day assessment school, we asked her, after her bedtime story:

"How do you think you'll feel in school tomorrow?"

Amelina thought for a moment and replied: "I think I'll be shy."

"Okay," Jørgen replied, adding: "How long do you want to be shy?"

It was clear that Amelina was a little surprised by this, as she looked at Jørgen, wondering, and said, after a long pause: "I'll be shy for an hour!"

"How will you feel when you're not shy anymore?" we asked.

Amelina lit up and said happily, "I will have fun".

"That sounds nice," we said – and then we talked about other things.

A little later in the conversation, Amelina stopped suddenly in the middle of a sentence and said, "No, I will only be shy for ten minutes!"

"And then you will have fun afterwards?" Mitzi asked, while Amelina nodded, affirmatively.

Jørgen had the pleasure of taking Amelina to school on the big day. On the way, he asked again how she thought she would feel, when she met all the new children who were older than her. Amelina thought for a moment and replied that she had decided not to be shy, but just to have fun all day and play with them all.

PARENTS ARE A BIT SLOW TO CATCH ON

I had a tight knot in my stomach on the way home, having left our little girl in a classroom with 22 children she did not know.

In the afternoon, when we went to pick up Amelina, we couldn't find her. We finally found her playing with three older girls, and she was reluctant to come home! On the way home, we asked her how her first day in school had been. Amelina looked at us tolerantly and said:

"It was really, really fun, and I played with all the children and I made loads of new friends."

It was obvious that she thought the question was a little silly, as she had clearly stated that morning how she would feel and how the day would go – it wasn't the first time she realised that her parents could be a bit slow to catch on.

Three days later, it came as no surprise to us when the class teacher enthusiastically told us that there was no doubt that Amelina was ready to go to school.

Something that got us thinking was that another little girl started the three-day assessment school with Amelina. We could see that she had unconsciously "chosen" to be shy on all three days and so was not allowed to start school until the following year.

This story is important for us because it is a good example of how, with a few tools, we as parents can create huge and important changes for our children; changes that have positive consequences over a lifetime. We will introduce you to these tools throughout the book.

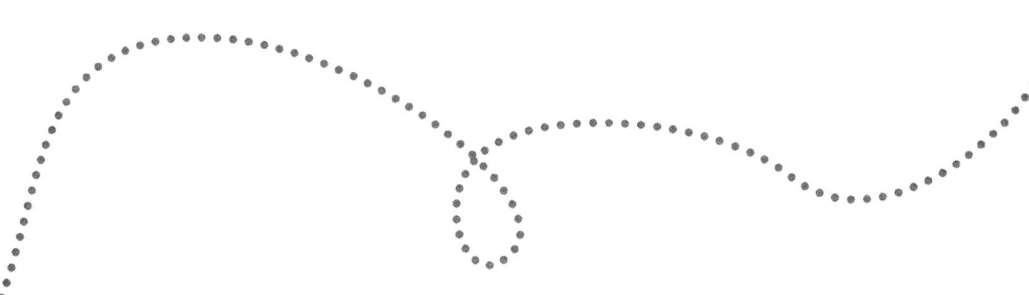

CORE BELIEFS

Our lives are paved with all we have been through and our experiences, good and bad. All this forms our core beliefs, which we use for guidance and navigation in life. You could say they are the rules that we follow. Some beliefs are conscious, such as when Jørgen decided that he would smell fish before eating it, after he once ate smelly fish and got sick! Other beliefs are unconscious. And Jørgen's experience with a smelly fish could have resulted in him not liking fish, without his being consciously aware of what had caused him to make that "decision".

The body or the brain creates an immediate, sensible decision based on experience. Significant or defining experiences that we have as children very often lead to unconscious beliefs because we, as children, are not necessarily able to connect our experiences with conscious decisions.

Fortunately, we do not know the future, but the story of Amelina's first day of school may well result in Amelina continuing to choose the strategy of having fun when meeting new people. Hopefully, she will go through life without shyness and with an openness towards meeting new people. The other little girl may have gone home with quite a different decision.

A HARMLESS REMARK BUT A GREAT EFFECT

That little girl's unconscious decision to be shy was not conducive to her starting school, but perhaps her decision was in relation to her taking care of herself. It may have been the girl's positive intention to choose shyness.

Let's try to imagine a situation where the little girl is sitting in the company of her parents and their friends. Let us imagine the parents telling their friends that their daughter must wait a year to go to school, "as she is always so shy."

Such an innocent remark can be disastrous. It cements the little girl's unconscious decision to choose shyness as a strategy, especially when it comes from the highest authority of all: the parents

It clearly ensures that the girl will choose shyness the next time she is in such a situation, for "she is always so shy!"

Thus, she can go through life shy about meeting new people – with all the inconveniences this can cause.

Now this scenario is, of course, a mere hypothesis, because we do not know the rest of the little girl's story, but through our work, for example in helping adults get over their shyness, we generally find that shyness starts at a very early stage in life; quite often due to a single event, which at the time did not seem particularly significant, but has since been so definitively cemented, again and again, that it has become a central part of the person's identity.

The key message here is that the things we say to our children have an overwhelming impact on their development and future life. On our journey through this book, we will share more examples that you might also recognise from your life as a parent. We will look at them in-depth and reveal the adverse effects they can have. Finally, we will give you some input into what you can say and do instead.

The things we say to our children have an overwhelming impact on their development.

THAT'S WHO I AM!

"You are so messy!"
"You never eat anything!"
"You're always late!"
"You're terrible at maths!"
"You never do as we say!"
"You always yell so loud!"
"You are so naughty!"
"You eat like a pig!"
"You are always so angry!"

Beliefs abound around us. They come in two varieties: the supportive and the limiting. Fortunately, we have many supportive beliefs. They are the ones that ensure we achieve what we want and act appropriately in life's different situations.

It is your own consciousness and decisions about which beliefs you want your children to have that are crucial for what beliefs your children receive. The work of putting those decisions into practice comes after this. We will show you how to do this later in the book.

WHERE DO THEY COME FROM?

Our beliefs often come from our own or others' experiences and, typically, our children inherit their beliefs from both their parents and other authority figures in their lives. Some beliefs are more amusing than others.

When we were children, we were told that we had to wait an hour after we had eaten before we could go swimming. Recently, Jørgen was teaching in Chile and he learned that they also have this rule – except they have to wait one hour and 15 minutes. The only problem with this belief is that it is false. There is no health-related reason as to why you should wait to go swimming after a meal.

It is an old – and apparently international – belief, which has survived for decades and has led to children, all over the world, sitting on beaches, perspiring, while they wait to be able to go and frolic in the sea. The belief may have arisen because in ancient times a child drowned after eating – or perhaps it is because dad just wants to have a nap after lunch? We don't know, but you yourself may know this belief and have practised it with your children.

A central part of this book deals with how we can identify the limiting beliefs that both we and our children are exposed to every day and how we can replace them with supportive beliefs, which can make life so much easier for our children. Our children can create their own obstacles in their own lives – they don't need us to help them create that baggage!

I AM SO SLOW

At one point during Amelina's time in infant class, Mitzi and I were told by the class teacher that Amelina was often the last to get dressed after gym. Maybe this was because she was younger than the others and, therefore, easily distracted if, for example, a fly flew past her coat rack. Or maybe not.

When we spoke to Amelina about it, she exclaimed: "Yes, I'm always so slow!"

Such an opinion got our belief-alarm-bell ringing (just as it certainly will with you, too, when you are finished on your journey with this book). Now, it's not a disaster to take your time getting dressed after gym, except that it challenges the gym teacher's patience. But suddenly we realised we had observed that Amelina was slow at eating her food. We may not have said that we thought she was slow at eating, but we had shown her that that was what we thought.

Children are so gifted that they not only hear every word we say, (even though we often think they don't), but they also "hear" everything that we don't say, everything we express in our body language, facial expressions and so on. We had probably unwittingly helped to plant a limiting belief about slowness in Amelina, a belief that could result in problems in the future.

Who does not remember those in the class who were always just 'slower' than the others at everything? We'd suggest that this was not due to weaker muscles or inferior intelligence; rather, to the belief that "that's who I am!"

HOW FAST WOULD YOU LIKE TO BE?

From that day on we did several things differently. First, we were very aware of not showing or saying to Amelina in any way that she was slow at anything. In addition, we challenged her emerging belief in three different but simple and effective ways.

The first opportunity presented itself one day, when Amelina was going to school and said, "Oh, we have gym today, and I'm always the last to get dressed."

"Oh," Mitzi said, and added, "Well, if you could choose, how fast would you like to be?"

Amelina lit up and said that she would be the fastest!

"Okay, what is it that prevents you from being the fastest?" Mitzi asked, casually.

"The fact that the others don't turn off the showers, so I have to do it, and so the others already have their clothes on when I'm starting to get dressed. "

That was it! The first important piece of information was obtained: an innocent outsider was causing something that was becoming an intrinsic limiting belief.

That issue with the showers could be solved in many ways without violating Amelina's sense of duty. Together we made a plan for how Amelina could both ensure that the showers were turned off and be the fastest at getting dressed.

The second opportunity presented itself a few days later: "I'm always so slow," said Amelina as she was putting on her shoes. Despite having solved the getting-dressed-situation in gym, the belief was still there. It had its own life – as do many of our beliefs. They are founded because of a need, but they are not necessarily removed when the need disappears.

WHEN THE BEST-BEFORE DATE IS EXCEEDED

You probably have some foods that you do not like. And then one day, you eat that food out of politeness and you discover that it actually tastes quite good. The reason is that, at some point in your life, you tasted a food (such as goat's cheese) that you did not like – either because of the preparation, the consistency, or maybe because of your taste buds' development at that time. Immediately, a belief was created that "I do not like goat's cheese." But cooking, texture and taste buds change, and, therefore, you could perhaps eat a different goat's cheese a month later with a different result, instead of eating it ten years later. The best-before date on beliefs can easily be exceeded.

Core beliefs were good for us on the day they were founded, but we "forgot" to "take them out of the fridge" after they exceeded their best-before date.

This was how Amelina could be the first to get dressed after gym, but still believe that she was "always so slow". We had to challenge that, and so when she was about to put on her shoes and would say that she was always so slow, we would ask her, "So what are you fast at?"

Amelina looked at us, irritated, but she could see the competitive element in the question, so before her shoes were put on and laced, she had already come up with an answer: she was fast at running, learning numbers, eating ice-cream and catching frogs.

Now we just had to ask her what she would choose to believe: that she was slow or, actually, that she was fast.

Amelina thought for a moment and then replied, "Well then, I'll be fast."

A new resolution, which meant a new belief was founded, and today, years later, Amelina still believes that she is fast at everything.

WHAT DOES YOUR CHILD BELIEVE ABOUT THEMSELVES?

Limiting beliefs come in many varieties and forms, and we all have many of them. In general, there are two types:

♦ The behaviour-related beliefs, such as "I never do anything right", "I am always late" and so on...

♦ The identity-based beliefs, such as "I'm messy", "I'm bad at languages" and so on ...

The identity-based beliefs can be particularly challenging, as we perceive our beliefs as truths. And who has not experienced how difficult it is to change a person who says "That's who I am!"?

The fact is that beliefs are not truths; they are our best guesses at truths. When we understand this, we realise that there are other truths. It gives us the opportunity to choose which "truth" will control our lives in the future.

There are some very simple techniques that we can use to identify beliefs and to deal with our children's limiting beliefs.

The fact is that beliefs are not truths; they are our best guesses at truths.

We should point out, however, that as a general rule it is not the parents' job to remove or alter children's beliefs. That is a battle in which we will be easily defeated, for those beliefs are theirs! As we see it, there is much more to responsible parenthood than simply a duty to challenge our children's beliefs.

Children should have the opportunity to choose whether they want to keep the beliefs they have or whether they want to make new ones that are more appropriate for them. And we believe completely that our children are capable of making such a choice.

FIND YOUR CHILD'S PREJUDICES

The first step is to become aware of what beliefs are – and to believe that they can be changed. The first time you support your children in changing a belief from a limiting one to a supportive one, your children have an experience that tells them that it is possible to change a belief. You will find that it is then much easier to do it again.

It is essential that you are able to identify core beliefs when you hear them. Here are some things you need to listen for carefully, so that core beliefs emerge by themselves:

Absolutes:	"I'm always ..." or "You never ..."
♦ Non-statements:	"I can't ..." or "I'm not ..."
♦ Position:	"They are stupid ..." or "It's hard ..."
♦ Prejudice:	"Girls say stupid things" or "The teachers don't listen to me"
♦ Generalizations:	"All the boys ..." or "You are always..."

And if you ask, "What stops you from ...?" – in relation to something your child would like to achieve – then your child's response is, by definition, also a limiting core belief.

If you have not thought about it before, direct your attention to the above linguistic statements of your children (and others). You will quickly find that a substantial part of the communication between people actually consists of core belief statements.

And if you consider that any of these statements can result in beliefs that we then carry through life, then it is probably easy for you to imagine how many stumbling blocks may come to be in your child's path.

Fortunately, it is easy to change limiting beliefs to supportive ones once we have identified them!

WHAT TO DO ABOUT CORE BELIEFS?

As you read in the examples of the first day of school and the gym-clothes issues, it requires just a simple question or statement from you to give your child the feeling that the core belief is not the final truth, and, therefore, can be changed if the child wants it to be changed.

There are various ways to deal with your child's beliefs. You will find that once you've had some practice with the different approaches, you will be in no doubt as to which method is the best for the situation with your child.

The fundamental issue is to challenge the core belief, which is often the opposite of what we choose to do.

Indeed, we basically have two normal – but unconscious – strategies for how we deal with our child's core belief statements, and both are counterproductive.

One strategy we use, for example, when a child is slow at getting dressed in the morning is to say, "Hurry up!" This only confirms the belief in the child that they are slow, and, therefore, contributes to maintaining the limiting beliefs.

TIME TO CHANGE STRATEGY

Often, the second strategy is to say: "You are always so slow!" Apart from this maintaining the limiting belief in the child, it simultaneously extends the belief that the only way to deal with getting dressed in the mornings is to use the absolute, "always." It is often said with great authority and a little irritation, which emphasises the seriousness of it. The result is that we tell the child that they are slow in all facets of life.

Therefore, you need to change strategy, and here is how:

♦ Knowledge of how incredibly important beliefs are for your child's well-being
♦ Awareness of the child's statements in daily life
♦ Awareness of how you feel in the situation, so instead of you using your old habit, you choose to say and do things differently
♦ Awareness of how you handle your child's statements

You can deal with the child's statements by using any one of the following tools.

REPEAT THE ARGUMENT

You can challenge the statement by literally repeating the limiting core belief clearly, so the child hears what they said. This way the child learns awareness of their habitual thinking. It is important that you do not say it as an emphasis of the child's statements, but more with a wondering or questioning tone.

Core beliefs work as self-fulfilling prophecies.

REFRAME THE BOUNDARIES

You can challenge these core belief statements by "reframing". To "reframe" means to move the frame or the boundaries. This way the child gets to see things from another perspective. For example, if the child says, "I am always so slow", then one way to reframe is by asking, "When you are not slow?" or "When are you fast?"

Firstly, it forces the child to change perspective from the limiting to the supportive, as the focus moves to situations where the child is quick. In that moment, when the child has identified such situations, it is an insight that "I am always so slow" is not true. Maybe you can help your child by saying, "Well, before you said that you were always slow. Now you're telling me about everything that you are fast at. How does that make sense with you always being slow?"

Another powerful effect of asking "When are you fast?" is that it contains a positive assumption. By framing the question in this way, we reveal to the child that we assume that there are things that the child is fast at, and we let the child discover them.

As parents, we want to create positive assumptions for our children, in order to show them that we believe in them. Without the positive assumption and supportive element, the question would sound something like this: "Is there something you're quick at?" To which the child will probably answer no, because "I'm always slow" is the core belief.

Other examples of "reframing" are:

♦ **None of the others like me!"** – "Who likes you?"

♦ **I'm not good at anything!"** – "What are you good at?"

♦ **Peter is always so annoying!"** – "When is he nice?"

CHALLENGE STATEMENTS

You can challenge statements by asking: "How do you know that?" You can typically do this with prejudices such as, "It will definitely be boring" or "He's guaranteed to be angry". The answer to how the child knows this could easily be, "Because he always is" – but then you are ready with a reframing.

You challenge this statement with the question: "When was it not like that?" This is a reframing that can be used in other circumstances. It requires a little practice. You can, for example, use it for absolutes or as the answer to the question "What stops you from...?" For example:

Child: "I'm *always* late."
Adult: "When are you not late?"
Child: "Em ... in school."
Adult: "So, how does that make sense – you are always late but you are on time for school?"

You may know a few of these classics, subconsciously; we tend to deal with them with an exasperated exhalation. Examples include:

"I can't remember" and "I don't know".

WE REMEMBER MORE THAN WE THINK

When Amelina was only two years old, we showed her some of the trees in our garden. We told her what they were called. Six months later, we pointed to a characteristic tree in the garden and asked her what kind of a tree it was. Amelina answered automatically that she could not remember. We challenged her with a reframed question: "What if we were playing a game where you could remember what kind of a tree it is?" Amelina was, of course, up for the game, and she replied, after a period of silence, with "Cherry", which was absolutely correct.

Here we have a basic limiting belief that is quite prevalent, namely the feeling that we cannot remember things, that we just do not remember or that we think we do not remember. Once we have decided that we cannot remember, then it is clear that we do not remember, because core beliefs work as self-fulfilling prophecies.

The brain is smart enough to stop trying to remember from that moment when we first tell ourselves and others that we do not remember.

IT'S BETTER TO HAVE A CHOICE

From our work with hypnosis, it is our firm belief and experience that we can actually remember everything that has happened in our lives. It's just stored deep down on the hard drive because there is not enough RAM to have it all readily available – but as it is on the hard drive, it can be found again. That is what hypnosis is all about. But you do not need to be hypnotised in order to find things that you thought you had forgotten. When we challenge "I do not remember" (in moderation, otherwise it could be quite annoying for the child), then we give the child a sense that they can remember something, quite well in fact, and which, of course, can be rewarding in all aspects of life – not least in school.

The basic philosophy when it comes to working with our children and their beliefs is that we believe that it is better to have a choice than not to have a choice. By challenging our child's core beliefs when we hear them, we give the child a sense that they have a choice and, therefore, that they can choose a belief that supports them over one that does not. That alone can create a huge positive change in the child's life trajectory.

In the next part of the book, we will explore how we can actively use supportive core beliefs in our relationships with our children.

FOCUS ON WHAT YOU WANT

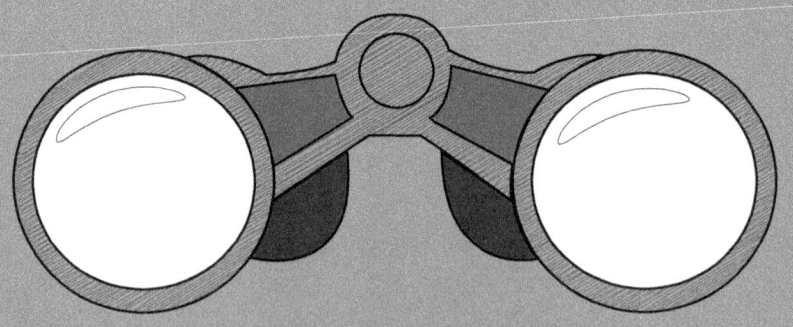

You come home exhausted from a rather challenging day at work. You think to yourself: you just won't be able to cope if the kids are short-tempered or bickering over everything from who gets to sit where at the dinner table to who gets to take an early bath.

The problem is that life often gives us exactly what we choose to focus on!

We always have a choice, and can, therefore, always choose to focus on the positive side of things. When the youngest child – annoyingly enough – knocks the eggs onto the floor again, think of it instead as a positive indication that they are eager to help with the cooking.

We are often very quick to tell our children what they should not do and what we do not want. If we instead try to let our children know what we do want, then we could, with very little effort, raise children who are motivated rather than discouraged from doing things.

And when children are motivated – when they know precisely what they want – they often benefit, and start accomplishing their goals. This is ultimately what drives your children, young or old.

THERE IS ROOM FOR POSITIVE INFLUENCES

In the chapter where we introduced the concept of core beliefs, we wrote down several statements that we often hear parents say to their children (see p. 29). Such statements, unconscious as they are, are still authoritative, and, therefore can limit the child. If they go unmonitored and are repeated frequently, parents can often lead the child to adopt the belief of the parent: surely it is easy to see that through enough repetition and being told by a parent 'you are messy', the parent's belief will be cemented into the child. The poor thing then has no alternative but to go through life being characterised as 'messy', and soon teachers, paediatricians, significant others and finally spouses will also confirm this trait – by then making the statement an absolute truth!

In much the same way, and just as effectively, you, the parent, can choose to give your children positive as well as supportive beliefs to carry throughout life, and these can become critical for their future success. After all, being messy is ultimately not the worst trait to have, but what about when a child thinks: "I'm useless?"

"

To give the
gift of
supportive
core beliefs
is fun.
So why
not start
today?

THERE IS ANOTHER VERSION OF REALITY

Now you are probably thinking that no parent could ever call their child useless, but they can and do! In fact, when working with adults, we often find them making such statements. If we, the authors, think back to our own childhood, one of us actually had a German teacher who was adamant that we were incapable of learning the language. The other was "enriched" by the beliefs of a Danish teacher who thought it best to remain uneducated. Not to mention the incident of a Danish physician who claimed that a ski-related knee injury, patched up in a small, local Italian hospital, would render one of us unable to dance again. Such examples of negative statements go on and on.

Today, when we find ourselves speaking German, dancing, and graduating from all kinds of educational programmes, our paradigms have been shifted. Situations have enabled us to look beyond the reality imposed by such derogatory statements.

> What authorities have you met in your life that have given you such "small gifts" in the form of limited assumptions?

Giving the gift of supportive core beliefs is both fun and beneficial, and you can quickly see the direct results of your efforts. So why not start today?

YOU ARE JUST SO GOOD AT THAT!

As mentioned earlier, parents ought to give their children the gift of supportive core beliefs to carry with them throughout life. Not only do they form behavioural guidelines, but they also represent truth to the child, in much the same way as the derogatory comments do. However, when we talk about giving supportive feedback, it is important to look at the issue of "praise", as that is something else entirely.

When we as parents, grandparents, paediatricians or teachers praise a child, saying for example that their drawing is great, we are in fact instigating the child's reaction. What usually follows is that the child immediately draws another picture in order to receive more praise. When a child has been praised for a particular action ten times a day for years, they soon identify themselves with that action – rather than with their own self. Therefore, the child runs the risk of having high confidence but low self-esteem.

The day the now-adult child no longer receives any recognition for their actions, their confidence will take a hit, and that adult could go through life with a self-esteem problem, often resulting in a large number of unhealthy patterns and conditions.

What you can choose to say to your child instead of praise, when they come to you with another somewhat indecipherable drawing, is:

"It's so nice to see how much you enjoy drawing."
"I can really see how much work you've put into this."

If you try out this technique tomorrow, you may notice that the words feel alien and artificial in your mouth. We can assure you that this feeling is temporary, and soon you will get used to commenting on your child's drawings and actions in this new way, thus strengthening their identity. The child will consequently associate your words with a feeling, rather than a reaction. Now you might think that all children should be praised, and don't worry, they will be. Try to notice how many people give your child praise – from grandparents to teachers. You will see that this new strategy will lead you to achieve a balance between praise that enhances confidence, and positive acknowledgement that strengthens identity and nourishes self-esteem.

In the short-term, praise is absolutely a form of a positive and supportive statement, but in the long-run it can act as a limitation. Therefore, it is important to carefully choose your positive statements so that your child's self-esteem – and not just their self-confidence – is supported.

WE BELIEVE IN THE GOOD

We have chosen two kinds of supportive beliefs for Amelina: ones which we believe support a good life, and ones which we believe will negate, over time, the limiting core beliefs that we have found in Amelina.

Amelina's Supportive Core Beliefs:
♦ You learn quickly
♦ You are a clever child
♦ You can learn everything
♦ You can play with everyone
♦ Life is good
♦ Life is easy
♦ You are careful
♦ You take good care of things
♦ We believe in the good

Amelina's Core Beliefs for Negating Limiting Beliefs:
♦ You are so quick at getting dressed
♦ You are good at remembering
♦ Every day can be a good day
♦ You choose your mood

When Amelina started in the first grade, she embarked on one of life's greatest projects: learning to read. Learning to read is vital for all further learning and for oral and written expression and communication. In other words, as long as we are talking about learning and professionalism, it is difficult to find anything more important. Like most children, Amelina thought it was fun and exciting to begin her exploration of letters and words. Yet, strangely, only some children continue to think it is exciting, while the rest lose interest.

LONG WORDS ARE THE EASIEST

Perhaps some children find reading easy because they are motivated to continue exploring and, therefore, quickly become quite good at reading. Those who find it difficult, meanwhile, are more prone to throwing in the towel early on and moving their focus onto something else. This means that it can be a year-long battle for the teachers, and it may be difficult to get the child to do their homework at home. From the beginning, Mitzi and I introduced a supportive core belief to Amelina that reading is easy, and we added casually: the longer the word, the easier it is! As rational parents, you might think that this is complete nonsense, and even if it is, we can still choose what we want to believe. And as long as it works, that is completely irrelevant.

The longer the word, the easier it is! 🙰

Actually, we can say that if it works, then no, it's not nonsense. Other parents in Amelina's class had unwittingly given their children other beliefs such as: "In first grade you should be able to learn fourletter words." As such, there is quite a high probability that that is precisely what their child learned in first grade. One day, Amelina went home with a classmate, and when the friend's father drove them home from school, he suddenly heard Amelina's voice from the back seat: "Co-pen-hag-en-Cen-tral-station". It was a sign that they passed whilst driving at 50 km per hour. Amelina firmly believes that reading is easy – and that long words are the easiest. You can, of course, choose which supportive beliefs are consistent with your values and outlook on life – and which ones you also believe will benefit your child as their own truth in life.

Don't despair if you are the kind of parent who is also human.

YOU HAVE HYPNOTISED
YOUR CHILD FOR YEARS

If you are under the misconception that hypnosis is something airy-fairy or only for people who want to stop smoking or overcome their arachnophobia, then you'd better take a deep breath and prepare yourself, because you are about to realise something: you have been hypnotising your child for years, probably without being aware of it!

Therefore, in this chapter, we will introduce you to how you have probably been hypnotising your child in everyday life, albeit unconsciously, and we will give you some ideas for how you can do it in a more appropriate manner.

Suggestions are central to hypnosis. They are one of the main techniques that make hypnosis a powerful development tool, whether it be for therapy, help with an addiction or overcoming a phobia.

A suggestion in hypnosis could be: "You will find that you are happy every time you see the colour red" or "You are no longer afraid of wasps". When the suggestion is made during a trance or a deeply relaxed state where our critical consciousness is "switched off", the hypnotised person can accept the suggestion. It is inserted into the mind as a "truth" – a little bit like the core beliefs we discussed in an earlier chapter. It happens automatically, and the more times the hypnotist repeats the same suggestion – and depending on how much authority the hypnotist has – the more the person will accept the suggestion and make it a reality.

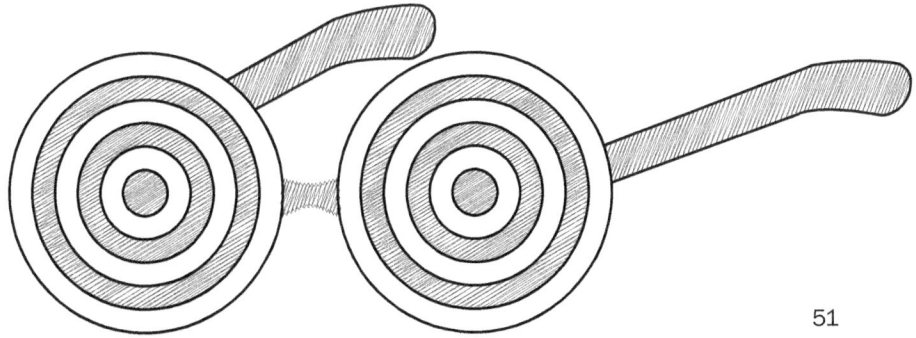

A CAR PARK FOR RESERVATIONS AND MISTRUST

This process is in fact extremely simple, and the key phrase here is "critical consciousness". Our critical consciousness is the only "enemy", for it is here where all our reservations, mistrust and experiences are parked. If someone stopped you in the supermarket and told you to purchase more oatmeal, chances are you would react in one of two ways: simply by rejecting the suggestion, or being slightly annoyed. This is why the hypnotist's trance is so vital – part of the consciousness is "switched off", which allows free access to what we call the subconscious. It is here that suggestions enter directly into our minds.

The hypnotist uses specific trance-inducing language to "turn off" the consciousness. There are many forms of trance language, but, typically it is a rhythmic, monotonous, chant-like language, which is difficult to listen to for long periods without losing concentration. Once concentration is lost, consciousness is put on hold – and the door to the subconscious mind opens wide.

We make the claim that on a daily basis – though without knowing it – you use hypnotic techniques in relation to your child, because studies have shown that consciousness is formed from the age of five to seven. Children below that age run around completely open to their world – to the suggestions they encounter on a daily basis. Moreover, you, as a parent, have more authority than any another person in your child's life.

A NEW BACKGROUND MUSIC

Imagine, therefore, what could happen if the inappropriate statements were eliminated during the child's first few years. Inappropriate statements are quite often formulated as "suggestions", which in turn are readily accepted by your child and lie in their subconscious mind as background music that determines what your child believes in, and their ideas about life.

When you repeat suggestions such as those listed below, again and again, with a tired and monotonous voice, you amplify the message each time until one day they are a fully integrated part of your child's identity.

"You use bad language!"
"You never clean your room!"
"You're always late with your homework!"
"You never finish your dinner!"
"You are unfair to your little brother!"
"You're always tired in the morning!"
"You eat like a pig!"
"Mathematics is certainly not for you!"
"You lie!"
"You are lazy!"
"You always quarrel with everyone!"
"You have to wait an hour before you go swimming after you have eaten!" (There's that one again!).

You can add your own "suggestions" to the list...

No one is free from having said stupid things to their children. We certainly can't deny it. So don't despair if you are the kind of parent who is human. Despite unconsciously using the above techniques to limit our child, we can, fortunately, also employ these same techniques to consciously support our children – and it's not too late to start now.

Here we have a unique opportunity to give our children those beliefs we would like them to hold, about themselves and the world.

You may find inspiration in the section on core beliefs (see p. 26-41). These techniques can be employed at times when your child is at their most susceptible to positive suggestion, such as just before bedtime (this also applies to older children, who have already formed their consciousness). At bedtime, your child is too tired to maintain concentration, and you may even be so tired yourself that your voice easily becomes monotonous and chant-like.

If you have small children, then you can see what happens if you say authoritatively to your child at bedtime:

"Now I will slowly count down from ten to one, and when I say one, you will immediately fall asleep! Ten, you become more and more relaxed ..." and so on through the countdown.

SUGAR WATER ALWAYS WORKS

There are other situations where you can – with great effectiveness – use conscious suggestions without crossing ethical boundaries in any way. Remember, you do it unconsciously anyway.

Some time ago, we had to pick up Amelina from a friend's house. There were four children in the garden and they were having great fun playing. Just as we arrived, one of the younger girls was stung by a wasp. She, of course, cried and cried, and her mother came running. When the girl sobbed that it really hurt, her mother uttered the following inappropriate suggestion, quite compassionately: "Yes, it really, really hurts when you're stung by a wasp!"

Jørgen fetched a bowl of water with a little sugar and let the mother dab it on the sting. Shortly afterwards, the girl's mother asked the girl if it helped. The girl naturally shook her head and kept on crying. Mitzi carefully entered the conversation and said, with all the authority she could muster: "Very soon the pain is going to disappear."

A few seconds later, she added: "Now the pain has stopped! Sugar water always works straight away!"

Instantly the girl stopped crying and resumed playing, while the parents continued talking. No one had discovered what she had done, because everyone believed in what she had said, as she said it so convincingly.

Actually, we have no idea whether sugar water works on wasp stings or not, but it worked anyway. It's probably not for nothing that we say that "faith can move mountains." And it's certainly not for nothing that for generations parents have kissed young children's scrapes and convincingly said that 'Now, it's better'. They did it because it works. But only a few know that it is hypnosis.

FEAR OF SNAKES AND SILENCE

Many phobias are limiting beliefs that have grown so great that in the worst cases they are debilitating.

Typical phobias are a fear of bugs, such as wasps and spiders, a fear of animals such as snakes, and a fear of places, such as heights, confinement and open spaces. In addition, there are also an endless number of little individual phobias, such as the fear of silence or the fear of how particular people look.

Common to most of these fears is that they are established in childhood. Typically, they are often, but not always, the result of a single traumatic event which led to an unconscious decision to be afraid of something. The belief stems from the person trying to protect themselves.

As parents, we don't have the power to prevent our children from developing a phobia at some point in life, but we have a greater influence than you might think.

As parents, we are incredibly good at transferring our own phobias to our children. Many children of parents who, for example, have a phobia of wasps will themselves develop a phobia of wasps, which can be restricting and highly frustrating – especially if you like to dine alfresco in August.

If the child, throughout their childhood, experiences that their mother or father is afraid of wasps, that fear is transferred to them, using exactly the same principle as when we transfer our linguistic affiliations.

If you do not want your children to inherit your phobias, then you can choose to keep them to yourself, and for yourself, from tomorrow.

Phobias can also intensify, causing lifelong discomfort and limited quality of life – but perhaps the time has finally come to eliminate them?

WHAT IS YOUR CHILD AFRAID OF?

On the other hand, you should not neglect your child's fears and phobias. Be aware of them and take your child seriously - even if it is something you are not afraid off or don't immediately understand as being scary.

Some time ago, Jørgen treated a woman for a wasp phobia. He discovered that the cause of the phobia was an experience she had, had as a child. When she was six years old, a wasp came in through the window of her parents' car. She was sitting in the back seat and was really scared. But her parents, who were not afraid of wasps, told her 'helpfully' from the front seat that she should relax. It was not what she needed in that situation, and the result of the 'innocent' episode was a wasp phobia, which was enforced and strengthened every time she saw a wasp over the years.

It is your own consciousness and decisions about which core beliefs you want your child to have that are crucial for the beliefs your child gets. You may inadvertently be creating undesirable beliefs if you show anxiety about something or if, at the other end of the scale, you choose not to care about what your child is afraid of.

The solution lies somewhere in between.

What are you afraid of?

How does your anxiety affect your child?

How long should it be like that?

What will you do differently?

MENTAL TRAINING CAN CHANGE YOUR LIFE

The principles and ideas we have shared with you in previous chapters are in fact collected in the personal development concept we, at *EmpowerMind*, call *"EmpowerMind Training"*. Indeed, it is the central premise that our company, *EmpowerMind*, is built on.

Over the past few years, we have had the pleasure of taking thousands of adults and young mental-athletes through a mental training programme with unparalleled results.

Mental training is based on the undeniable fact that what we hear shapes our lives. This happens through the power of suggestion, which works regardless of whether we make the suggestions to ourselves or others make them to us. All that is required to get the optimum effects of beneficial suggestion is for the critical consciousness to be turned off. Therefore, mental training's first phase is to identify the so-called "alternative state of consciousness", where the subconscious mind is most receptive to positive re-programming. From this basis, we have developed a variety of custom mental training programmes, which provide suggestions for influencing the subconscious mind – both in children and adults. If you google *"EmpowerMindShop"*, you can try it out on your children. There is a guaranteed effect regardless of whether it's about being better at maths, sleeping better at night, escaping stress and worries, being more focused or having an increased "whatever-limit". There are many possibilities. The only requirement is that you sit or lie down for 15 minutes on the couch daily and listen to your inner self. How hard does that sound?

WE ALWAYS HAVE A CHOICE

A number of years ago, Jørgen was convinced that he was who he was; that he was born with a number of characteristics that couldn't be changed. As a matter of fact, he didn't even consider the possibility of change: there's no reason to when there's nothing you either want to or can change!

Through our work, we realised that beliefs change over time, and equally as important, that we could change them at will. Today, we view our lives as creations that we create ourselves – and, therefore, we can re-design ourselves, if we feel the need.

Previously, Jørgen was also convinced that emotions came from outside him, that it was others that made him mad, happy or frustrated. Most people we meet in everyday life experience the same thing, this idea that they are only in control of their feelings to a certain extent.

> If you also believe this, then we would like to challenge you by asking: who determines the emotions that affect you?

The answer is inevitable, though it may be difficult to accept. There is only one person who is 100% responsible for the emotions that affect you – and that's you.

This means that if someone acts unjustly towards you, then it is you who chooses to react with anger and, likewise, if someone says something nice to you, it is you who chooses to feel joy!

Once you accept this premise, it opens the way for the natural consequence: if it's me who is 100% responsible for the feelings I have in the world, then it is also possible for me to choose the feelings I want!

Now there may be some people reading this who are thinking that this is impossible – feelings are just what happen to you in certain circumstances. Yes, they happen because you allow them to happen – that's the only reason!

When you have also accepted this premise, there is only one question left: how would you like to be? Do you want to be angry, happy, irritated, upset, sad – or something completely different?

Most of us go through life on emotional auto-pilot, and accept all of the outside influences that we are exposed to. These influences are uncritically allowed to elicit emotions in us – emotions which are not necessarily beneficial for us.

Some may think that this is the very essence of being human; it separates us from the animals. But then a blackbird is more gifted than a human. For when did you last meet an angry blackbird that flew around with a little black cloud over his head, scolding all his friends with a shrill whistle?

We believe that evolution has given us the gift of emotions; a gift that means that we can enjoy a sunset or feel the surge of love. And we are only now beginning to come to the realisation that we can control our emotions and, thereby, choose those that are best for us.

Indeed, it is well-documented that negative emotions create physical blockages in the brain that hinder chemical substances which are beneficial to us, the endorphins, from passing freely. This causes us to age faster and be more vulnerable to a variety of diseases. Therefore, a shortcut to good health and a long life is to choose to fill our lives with good, positive feelings. It's also more fun!

As we now know, there is no reason to hide this good news from your children. As a parent, you can easily tell the above to your child with a good chance that they will understand – maybe they will understand it even better than you do, because your child is not affected by a lifetime of experience that feelings "are just something that happen" to us. And yet, it is uncertain if it will work if and when your child is exposed to a stimulus that unknowingly sets off their emotions.

TURN ON YOUR MOOD BOX

Mitzi and I thought long and hard about how we should use our knowledge in relation to four-year old Amelina, who was characterised by a sunny temperament. It was a good friend who came up with the idea. One day he told us about a small device he had designed with two buttons, one with a grumpy smiley face and one with a happy smiley face. We promptly accepted the idea, went home and whipped up a little electronic device for the first time since elementary school. The result was three matchbox-sized mood boxes. Each had a battery inside and a toggle switch with two positions, one that lit a little green light and one that lit a little red light.

It was time to introduce the box to the family. The idea was that when we got up in the mornings, we had to choose whether it would be a happy day or a grumpy day by switching the toggle over to the little green or little red light.

Naturally, it worked from day one – who gets up in the morning and thinks: "I'm going to be so grumpy today!"

Amelina thought it was really funny, and her little box stood, day after day, in her room, glowing green.

Then, when it occasionally happened that Amelina was upset about something, we would just ask her how long she thought she would be upset, and if she wanted, we could change her mood box to red. This was usually sufficient for Amelina to quickly change her mood, despite her being less susceptible to suggestions when she is angry, especially from her father, who has almost unlimited energy.

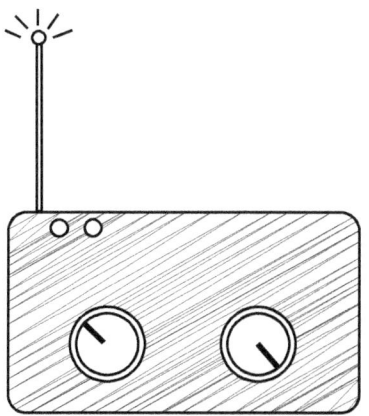

WHAT MAKES YOU ANGRY?

Amelina now knows that she manages her mood and her feelings. And, although, she obviously experiences vexing feelings just like everyone else, she has basically chosen to be happy.

A simple question you can ask your child is: "Yesterday, you chose to sulk for all of dinner. How long are you going to sulk the next time you are annoyed?"

This question has some built-in enhancing assumptions that often work better than directly saying that you can choose your feelings. We use the words "you chose", which of course imply that it was something the child selected – but the child is not necessarily aware of this.

We use the words "how long", which imply that the duration of the anger is a free choice.

Another slightly more complex question might be: "What is the advantage of being angry?" A follow-up question to the answer would then be: "What can you choose next time that gives you the same result but which is nicer for you?"

The built-in assumption in the question is that we do nothing without a positive intention; it gives us something. At the same time, the premise that we can do other things that give us the same result is also built-in. And again there is the built-in assumption that we have a free choice, which is perhaps the most powerful insight we can pass on to our children. Try it and see what happens!

> What mood do you want to choose from this moment on?
>
> What percentage of your day is it acceptable for you to be in a particular mood?
>
> What can you do to remind yourself that you have taken responsibility for your own mood?

MISTAKES ARE GREAT

One of the things we have learned through supporting development processes in adults is that we live in an anti-failure culture, in the sense that we feel that mistakes are bad.

It is no wonder that we view things this way, as throughout life we are praised when we do something good, and scolded when we do something wrong.

Here, we humans are not much different from rats. If we are rewarded we do more of what we did, in order to be rewarded again. And we strive to avoid and cease doing what we were scolded for.

In many ways this is appropriate; if it was not for the fact that we also learn that mistakes are bad for us and not worth remembering.

The danger of this distinction is that we, therefore, aim to play on the safe side in life and so we limit our ability to develop outside the secure area.

In reality this is not a problem, but rather an opportunity to learn more about ourselves that we do not take enough advantage of. It is during these times that our understanding of and insight into ourselves and new experiences expands. This new level of understanding and insight then remains with us when we attempt new things that we expect will succeed.

MISTAKES ARE POSSIBILITIES FOR LEARNING SOMETHING NEW

Our mistakes are actually opportunities that we do not utilise sufficiently. The difficulty with our anti-failure culture is that many people experience and view failure as fiascos.

From this follows the belief that the more mistakes we make in life, the greater tendency we have to see ourselves as a failure.

> *It is you exclusively who decides whether your child sees themselves as a failure when they make a mistake. It depends entirely on how you deal with it.*

We have all witnessed parents scolding their children for knocking over a glass of milk at the dinner table or for not doing what was expected of them.

It can, of course, be the final straw that the table cloth has to be washed for the fifth time in a week. But it is actually worse for the child if they are continuously scolded for wasting good milk, as it confirms their belief that they are not worth anything – meaning that the child has yet another building block for their Ministry of Poor Self-Esteem.

WHAT CAN YOU DO DIFFERENTLY NEXT TIME?

What is perhaps even worse than this (if there is anything worse) is that the child does not learn "not to spill".

Rather, a natural reaction for the child is to say to themselves at the next meal: "I must not spill, I can't waste milk", with the consequence that the child spills the milk again.

As parents, we can choose a different strategy.

The next time the milk is knocked over, you turn the other cheek and ask kindly, "what happened?"

Your child will wonder a little about the (stupid!) question and perhaps indulgently tell you that the milk was spilled. Your next question will bring your child to a reflective mode, where they become a little smarter.

"What did you do that caused the milk to spill?"

Your child will probably think for a moment and explain exactly what happened. Now your child will learn cause and effect. Your third question is the key question:

"What will you do differently next time?"

The answer to that question is a new strategy devised by your child, and you can stop using it if it doesn't work.

By addressing the situation in this style, your child benefits in a number of ways: firstly, they learn that mistakes do not equal failure. Secondly, it teaches your child about their "mistake". Thirdly, your child takes ownership of a new strategy, which is the crucial point. It is much more effective than the child learning what they should and shouldn't do.

This means that the next time the milk is knocked over for the same reason (if it happens at all again!), you can confront the child with an observation:

"I see that the milk was knocked over because it was too close to the edge of the table, even though you said you would place it further in on the table. What can you do differently next time?"

When the child then says the same thing as before, then you can say, for example:

"So, what can help you remember to do what you decided you would do before?"

NO FIASCOS HERE

With a little practice, you can get really good at turning mistakes into effective lessons. It is actually much more fun than getting angry. You will find that it works on lots of other things and not just spilled milk!

On our fridge, we have a little note that says: "No fiascos here – only lessons!" The note is liberating to look at from time to time, especially if we have forgotten that idea for a moment!

> How do you view making mistakes?
> How do you deal with your child when they make a mistake?
> What will you do differently from tomorrow onwards?

YOU GET WHAT YOU FOCUS ON

Have you ever wondered about the way that your predictions often come true? Imagine you are travelling home from your holiday by car, and before the journey, you say to yourself that the children will most likely be impatient and quarrel with each other when you're stuck in traffic on the motorway. Well, you've probably predicted the outcome of your journey.

Or picture this scenario: you are hosting a child's birthday party and you tell your partner that it will probably get rather chaotic with all the children, especially with the neighbours' boundary-pushing kids in attendance. It will probably be one of those parties where you are constantly interrupted with questions from the children about how to play a game, which under ordinary circumstances they are quite capable of playing.

Subsequently, you may wonder what others think of the birthday party – perhaps, they will offer the opinion that it was a great party with never a dull moment.

The law of attraction is in play here. It has only one, short and sweet, clause: you get what you focus on!

Some time ago, we went on a little skiing trip to Sweden, so Amelina could get her first taste of the slopes. While there, Mitzi and I had cause for alarm when Amelina, after a series of violent crashes on the top of the mountain in dense fog, cried and exclaimed: "This is the worst day of my life!"

We recognised that this was not an appropriate time to try some of the above techniques with Amelina. Instead, we helped and comforted her in the best way we could, and minutes later, she whizzed down a sunlit mountainside in high spirits. You also need to be aware and sensitive of your child's emotional state after an incident that has deeply affected them. That is not the time to say clever things to your child. Actually, that's like waving a red flag to a bull.

You get what you focus on! 🙶

It is, however, very important to take up the incident at a later date and talk it through at your leisure when all parties feel they are able to do so. If you do not already have experience of this, you will probably be pleasantly surprised at how clever your child is in such situations.

Later in the day, we reminded Amelina about the law of focus, which she had been introduced to several years earlier. She could easily see her reaction was inappropriate. Amelina thought about how she could do things differently next time she was in a bind.

RELEASE A HUGE POTENTIAL

Although the law is short and sweet, the effect of the law of focus contributes greatly to whether your child's day is good or bad.

For instance, you may choose to focus on the negative outcome of a particular event, because you have experienced a similar event in your past which resulted in a negative outcome, and this negative outcome now forms part of your baggage. You are most likely un-aware of it, but if you take time to reflect, the original negative experience may come to mind.

Since it is virtually impossible to go through life without negative experiences, it is important to talk about the negative experiences your child has. It gives the child an opportunity to understand that it is not a natural law that determines whether negative experiences lead automatically to similar negative experiences in the future; rather, it is the child's own decision about the outcome, which is crucial for which attributes it will have.

The law of focus applies in all aspects of life.

That is a vital piece of information when you are choosing what you want to focus on. It is also worth noting that thoughts and statements are self-reinforcing. This combination of the law of focus and self-reinforcing statements can put an effective limit on anything – or it can unleash tremendous potential for your child and yourself: you get what you focus on!

Just think of everyday statements such as: "The weather is awful", "It's boring",

"I'm not good enough", or a little innocent "It's hard" or "I'm so busy." And then there is the classic:

"We won't make it!"

When we introduced the law of focus to Amelina, we explained to her that it is much more beneficial to believe in possibilities, instead of limitations. As Amelina was only three years old at the time, we were not sure if she had understood, but what if she had...

YOU HAVE TO BELIEVE DAD

A sunny Friday in December, shortly before her fourth birthday., Amelina and Jørgen enjoyed the pleasure of a father-daughter day. They made an ambitious plan for the day: fun activities and some chores. Amelina loves drawing and so she drew all the things they had planned, in order , according to how she believed and wanted them to turn out. They headed off when she was finished.

One of the items they had planned was to have lunch in a fast food restaurant, and some hours later as they sat there and ate - or rather, as Jørgen sat there and ate, while Amelina crawled around in the legendary plastic tube high up near the ceiling and only sporadically came down to grab a bite of her food - time passed. Jørgen sat and counted the hours needed for their plan, which was only half completed.

Experience told him it would be of great advantage to employ the "preframe" technique: he should prepare Amelina for making changes to the plan in order to avoid conflict. So the next time Amelina passed by with happiness shining out of every pore and sweaty hair, he said to her, "Amelina, there is something we have to talk about. Unfortunately, we can't stay here playing for this long, and still have time to collect the trailer, drive to the recycling centre, see the Christmas fair at the shopping centre and then go home and put the roast pork in the oven before Mum comes home from work!"

Amelina took a break from sucking her straw, looked at Jørgen over the rim of her drink, and said kindly, but convincingly, "Dad, you have to believe that we CAN do it!"

Amelina looked at Jørgen expectantly and challengingly. He had no choice. So soon afterwards, the pair were in full swing, completing the rest of the plan – and needless to say, the roast was in the oven when Mitzi came home.

This story has become part of Amelina's tale, and it is good to return to when there have been other situations where Amelina needs to be reminded of the law of focus in an effective way – just like when we were skiing in Sweden.

What do you focus on in your family?
In theory?
... And in practice?

POSITIVE WORDING

Positive wording is the key to the law of focus. There is a good reason for this: the brain cannot understand the word "no". Define what you want to achieve instead of focusing on what you want to avoid!

Let us try a little experiment: Right now, I DON'T want you to think about a cheese sandwich!

Did you think of a cheese sandwich? It is nearly impossible not to think of a cheese sandwich, just for a brief moment. This is the law of focus again – you get what you focus on.

The cheese sandwich exercise is pretty innocent, but think about the following statements:

"You must not spill beetroot on your white blouse."
"You must not fall and get your trousers wet."
"Do not talk with your mouth full."
And so on, and so forth.

It is quite remarkable how often we as parents tell our children what they should not do, instead of telling them what they should and may do.

Firstly, it means that they focus on what they should not do, which is far more difficult than focusing on what they should do. Secondly, we get them used to expressing what they want to avoid, instead of defining what they want to achieve. We see this, too, in most adults who are very capable of defining and explaining what they do not want, rather than expressing what they do want.

The law of focus is as effective as the law of gravity: expressing what you want to avoid effectively results in you getting more of what you do not want.

The law of focus is just as effective as the law *of gravity: expressing what you want to avoid effectively results in you getting more of what you want to avoid.*

"THROW OUT THE WORD "NOT"

Last year, the teachers at Amelina's school were on a day course, and the parents acted as substitutes for the entire day. Jørgen was one of the lucky ones who got a few hours with the children, and one of his tasks was to remind them of the rules of the road before they set off for the train station to go to a museum. He asked the class what the children should remember, and a sea of hands skyrocketed into the air: "We can't go out on the road", "We can't let go of each other's hands", "we must not cross the road on a red man", "we must not fight and push each other", "we can't....". Not one of them knew what they should do, but all knew what they should not do. His task, therefore, was to turn all these negative statements on their heads, just as we do with Amelina when we become aware of negatively focused statements .

"When you are not allowed to go out on the road, what should you do?.

"We have to stay on the footpath".

"Yes, exactly, you stay on the footpath!"

The formula is simple: ask "when you do not...what do/should you do?" Then you get the positive version, which you anchor by repeating it clearly and with the same words.

This way, your child becomes used to formulating positive statements. They are much more appropriate and beneficial for the law of focus.

Now you just have to remember to tell your child what they should and may do, instead of what they shouldn't do. A penny for each "no", and next year's summer holiday is almost fully funded in most homes!

> **Try counting the "nots" in a week: Draw lines on the refrigerator with a redboard-marker - and see which one of you is heading for "victory".**

TELL YOUR CHILD WHAT IS GOING TO HAPPEN

Preframing is a term that refers to "setting a framework" for something before it occurs. For instance, we often receive an agenda or a plan for a course we are participating in or a party we are attending. It works for us adults. It makes us relax, reduces our expectations and helps us to get an overview.

Preframing also has a positive effect on children. They thrive on knowing what will happen next. I'm sure you have been on the receiving end of the result of saying to your child, 'Time for bed now!' just as they are in the middle of something! The thing is - children are, naturally, always in the middle of some specific game, they are in the middle of finding out which game to start playing next.

But if you preframe all the potentially difficult time, like dining, bedtime, going out of the door or turning off the computer, then it will be much, much easier. You are no doubt also well aware of this - all it requires is that we, as parents, have enough energy to provide these service announcements, five, 10 or 20 minutes before the event. The result is a child who feels respeted.

If you are in doubt as to whether or not you have the energy to give these service messages, a relevant question is:

Why is it that what your child has decided to do is less relevant, than what you have decided they should do?

PEACE FROM ADULT-LIKE WHIMS

Have you ever wondered why young children thrive on predictability, but for adults it can be quite dull? Children love rituals: they will read the same bedtime stories over and over again, and they do not stay awake at night thinking about new ways to serve their favourite dish.

The explanation is simple: they want to be able to predict what will happen so they can use their energy to be present, so that they can figure out what to do. It makes them feel safe.

In our everyday life, we have lots of nonverbal preframing. In Denmark, for example, it happens for most families, Friday after Friday, when the children know that after dinner there is Disney Club on the TV. This means that – without talking about it – we know that we collapse onto the sofa, cuddle, make small talk and have fun with Friday chocolate and red wine. There is peace from checking emails, combing lice and other adult-like tasks. Basically, the cartoons are not that important, but the framework is predictably set for us to enjoy ourselves together.

Preframing also works for big and new events in children's lives.

CAN CHILDREN CLIMB MOUNTAINS?

During the summer, Amelina and Jørgen were on vacation in the Mont Blanc region. It was a hiking trip where we would have to hike between 7 and 14 km a day in order to reach the base-camps where we could get food and shelter. The trip took us from valleys to mountain passes with thousands of metres of height difference every day.

Amelina was six years old at the time, and when I told people about the plan, they replied unequivocally that their children would never be able to do that. We, however, were convinced that Amelina could do it.

A hiking holiday had been suggested six months earlier, and it was Amelina herself who had decided that it should be through mountains and not through forests. We worked hard to explain to Amelina exactly what the trip entailed, even though we knew she had no chance of evaluating it in relation to her abilities and stamina. In the months leading up to our departure, when Amelina and Jørgen chatted together, he described in detail how they would have to hike from morning to night only taking breaks when they wanted to. He challenged her by asking her if she thought she could handle that. Amelina was in no doubt that she could. We briefly considered bringing tents for an emergency night in the open, but we were confident she could do it.

One beautiful afternoon in July, the train rolled in from Geneva into Chamonix after a wonderful trip over part of Mont Blanc. Our hiking adventure was to start the next day, and we were ready.

Children love rituals, they will read the same bedtime stories over and over again and they do not stay awake at night thinking about new ways to serve their favorite dish.

NO MOUNTAIN TOP WITHOUT *PREFRAMING*

At 6:30 the next morning, we left our apartment and headed for the first summit. Ten hours, 3,000 vertical metres and 24 kilometres later, we reached our lodgings for the night. As Jørgen lay gasping on the grass in front of the beautifully located retreat with swollen feet and the sound of clanging cow bells in his inner ear, Amelina was running around happily, playing with the children who lived there – for hours!

So he decided to increase the ambition for the following day and chose a higher route than we'd ever imagined she could handle. And again, it was Amelina who insisted on going a little further that afternoon to reach a glacial river where we could wash off the dust.

Of course she could handle it. Children use 100% more energy than adults on a normal day, and they have unlimited resources.

However, we are absolutely certain that she could not have climbed the first peak without preframing. We had only to think of the countless everyday 20-minute walks, where she, at least eight times, asks, 'Are we there yet?' Imagine if preframing also worked there…

Where in your life could you earn some quick brownie points for your harmony account by "preframing" things a little more clearly?

VALUES

The word "values" is tossed around a lot today. Indeed, self-respecting businesses characterise their businesses with values such as quality, integrity and service. We often see them stated and framed in the reception area.

Those are not the kind of values we are talking about here. We are talking about values that inspire and drive us.

For a great many of us, our values are unconsciously embedded in all that we do and make through life. They can change over the years, though some are more fundamental than others. We call these core values. The difference between values and core values is that while values may well vary from situation to situation, core values remain steadfast.

There are three advantages in being aware of values. Firstly, it makes us more aware of why it is important for us to achieve something in particular, and, thereby, it gives us extra drive to move in the right direction. Secondly, when we review our values, we ensure that what we are aiming towards is something we definitely want, and not just something we think we want. Thirdly, by linking our values to something we want to achieve, we actually anchor the belief that it is an important objective. In other words, our values provide strong motivation that we can actively apply in our lives – when we are aware that they exist.

"
We are talking about values that inspire and drive us.

VALUES ENSURE MOTIVATION

Discovering another person's values is easy, it's just a different process than we think it is. If you ask someone directly what their values are, they will often respond with what they rationally think are their values. However, there is a different and more effective way to discover their values, and that method can also be easily applied to your children to ensure their motivation and drive in the big and small everyday trials, such as homework.

When Amelina was two years old, we learned something we will never forget. We were sitting by the lake in the garden. The sun was shining and autumn's brown reeds were reflecting in the surface of the water, so the water shone like gold. We were sitting on a tree trunk, eating biscuits and drinking chocolate milk, and it was one of the first times that we had a great talk with Amelina. Amelina was just finding out about formulating longer sentences and was surprised by her new ability, and, without any ulterior motive, Jørgen asked Amelina what she would like to be when she grew up.

Amelina thought for a moment and replied: "I would like to be a super girl!"

"A super girl?" he repeated, surprised.

"Yes," said Amelina, and looked up: "Kinda like a doctor, someone who helps others!"

"Okay," replied Jørgen.

We were silent for a moment, as a heron landed out on the lake. A conflict raged inside Jørgen: should he challenge her with a question that even many adults find difficult to answer, or should he keep quiet and not ruin the moment?

DO NOT UNDERESTIMATE YOUR CHILDREN

He made a quick decision, turned to Amelina, who sat watching the heron that was standing perfectly still and attentive in the water up to its knees, and asked:

"Amelina when you're a super girl – such as a doctor, someone who helps others – what does it give you?" he asked, although he immediately regretted it. Damn our excessive ambition on our child's behalf!

Amelina looked at us for a while, and as we watched her, we saw how she was unsure for a moment, as she sought for a word.

"Ha ... happy," she said at last and smiled broadly as she nodded, agreeing.

In that second, Amelina put any doubts we had to shame. Despite an incredibly immature brain and an immensely limited vocabulary, it was Amelina who found the value that was tied to her wish for the future.

It was the first time that we saw – and realised – that children can do much more than we give them credit for. Since that day we have never made the mistake of underestimating our daughter!

A positive bonus was that Amelina, at a very young age, learned that something she wanted to achieve would give her a feeling if she achieved it, and she remembers this very important lesson. It formed a foundation on which to build.

A REMINDER FOR THE FUTURE

When we put values on what we want to achieve, we create an emotional anchor, which is experienced as a reminder for the future.

Think about when you come across an old holiday photo. The moment you set eyes on it, the whole experience comes back to you in detail – sometimes with emotions, smells or a particular piece of music.

That's what a good reminder can do.

It's easy to create reminders for the future. You don't even need a camera to take a picture. The brain is capable of doing it all by itself.

The advantage of having reminders for the future is that they, just like holiday photos in the drawer, are not forgotten. They can be used as unconscious markers for setting a direction that is in accordance with our values. Therefore, reminders are good for us.

All you need to do in relation to the story about Amelina on the tree trunk is to add an extra level of abstraction. It requires maybe (maybe!) slightly more life experience than two years can give.

It is easy to make reminders for the future

The key is imagining.

Next time you sit down with your child, who might not want to do their homework, try a different strategy than the one you have tried so far. The strategy consists of two steps: a performance and a question.

Imagine that you are sitting in school tomorrow morning, and you have all your homework done, so when the teacher asks you a question, you can answer it.

What does it give you?
What more does it give you?

Step 1 gives rise to the notion of desired conditions in the future, in this case, just tomorrow, but it could also be in a year or in ten years. Step 2 asks for the value behind the thing you want, and if you ask the same question over and over again, you get deeper into the values. A memory for the future is created.

YOUR CHILD CONSTRUCTS THEIR OWN LIFE

Imagine a building site with a wealth of building materials: bricks, beams, roof tiles and plenty of sand and cement. After some construction work, all the parts have become a building. Perhaps it will be a house, a castle, a church or a prison; perhaps a bridge, or a tower. Maybe the building will be beautiful, maybe boring, or just ugly.

We can't figure that out by looking at the building materials. We may get an indication, but we can't be certain without the architectural drawings.

We construct our lives in the same way. So when the child builds their building, they mix their own experiences, beliefs and attitudes with those of their parents, teachers, friends and all the other people that the child comes into contact with.

How the building will look is only one aspect – its height, form, number of windows and so on. We can perhaps agree on that. But how it is experienced is something else entirely. Some will think it is ugly, while others will think it is splendid. It is all in the eye of the beholder, and so it is with our lives.

We see our life as we have decided to see it. Others may well see it differently. You may know the feeling that you think you're lazy, while others feel you are energetic, or that you think you're ugly, but others find you beautiful.

OH, IT'S NOT BLEEDING?

Our children construct their lives, and depending on where they put the "windows" and how many odd angles they build, they will get a view of themselves that they will then carry with them through life. Their belief about themselves is based upon how you feel about your child. Later, it is based on their perception of themselves, in which your and others' perceptions of them have been included in the decision-making process.

Therefore, it is important that we as parents, at an early stage, discuss with each other the values that are important to our families – and, of course, support them in our thoughts, speech and actions, so they can flourish in our new families.

Friends of ours have often expressed a desire for their child to grow up to be independent and able to make brave, fair decisions. Yet, at the same time, they rush to help the child whenever he or she falls, worrying unnecessarily and comforting an otherwise unharmed child.

Children learn quickly. And most children – like most adults – like attention. Therefore, it does not take long for the child to learn to cry a little harder after a fall to ensure that they get attention faster.

We are sure you can figure out how the care-giving attitude of the parents here' supports or impedes their desire to have an independent and courageous child.

Few children are harmed by falling. A fragile self-image is far more detrimental.

DO WE TRY TO BE INDISPENSIBLE?

When Amelina was born, we discussed how we thought she should think about herself and what characteristics we wanted her to develop. Independence and resilience were some of them, and it has had the consequence that we have developed increased parental resilience.

To bring our thoughts to fruition, we forced ourselves not to mollycoddle her, but to be balanced, patient, confident and strong, and always loving and empathetic. This applied, for example, when Amelina was 2 years old and enjoyed climbing. She wanted to climb high, but her skills were still uncertain, so she fell off the climbing frame, trees and chairs, fell over her own and others'' feet, and became well-acquainted with the sitting room's wood-burning stove.

One summer when Amelina was 3 years old, we were sitting, after a canoe trip, eating fish from the campsite's barbeque. Suddenly, we saw Amelina in the distance climbing up over the monkey bars, which are intended for older children to swing on. It was easily well over a two-metre fall to the asphalt, and the gaps between the bars were wide enough for her to fall through.

The lifeless fish hung on our forks in mid-air, as we watched with trepidation as Amelina crossed what was in our hearts a rope-bridge at Niagara Falls.

Of course she did it, and had a new found core belief:

"I'm younger and smaller than all the others, but I can climb higher and don't fall down."

Saying that our little ones should learn from their own experiences is easy enough; allowing them to do it is not so easy. Most parents agree that we do our children a disservice by "saving" them from life's challenges – and, in reality, we may actually achieve the complete opposite of what we really want.

However, it is in the face of everyday life that we must prove that we do actually believe in what we say we want, to each other and to our children. Every day offers new challenges that our children encounter and safely come through, if we allow them to: cycling to school or to a playmate's house alone, taking the bus by themselves, being home alone, having the key to the house, etc...

Today, Amelina is a resilient girl who only cries when it really hurts   -
or when she's madd or sad. Amelina has a glorious, and childish, feeling
that she is good at everything, not because we have said that she is
clever, but because we have shown it to her with confidence.

Few children are harmed by falling. Indeed, a fragile self-image is
far more detrimental for them, as it leads them to believe that they
cannot handle something by themselves.They come to believe this
because their parents have not shown them confidence. Maybe this is
because the parents need to be needed - and, therebymake themselves
indispensable?

If, along the way, you nedd moral support, think of the competent
teachers who are professionally and lovingly dealing with your child
through the many potentially dangerous challenges of kindergarten
and school. Most children survive!

How would you like your children to experience and see themselves
as adults?

What are the consequences for the way you deal with your children?

GIVE YOUR CHILD MORE RESPONSIBILITY IN EVERYDAY LIFE

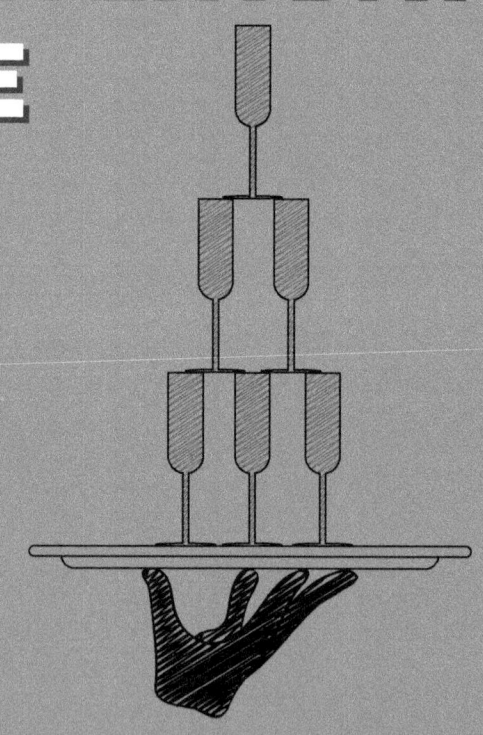

With the best of intentions, we fill our children full of instructions on how to live a good life. This results in creating externally-controlled children who have a lot of self-confidence, but not necessarily high self-esteem, as they cannot feel who they are or what they would like. They have low self-esteem because they are acknow-ledged more for their actions than for the person they are. When we praise a child's beautiful drawings and automatically display them on the refrigerator, we boost self-confidence – not self-esteem.

We believe we can wholeheartedly trust that children can take responsibility for and ownership of many things in their lives; how else can children feel when they are tired, if we, as parents, tell them when to go to bed all their lives?

As humans, we thrive when we take responsibility for our own lives – although it is easier when we don't! We do not want our children to hand over responsibility for their lives to others with a "what do you think?" attitude when they are grown. We all want independent sons and daughters who are capable of feeling what makes sense for them – and who are able to then express that.

CHARM, CONFIDENCE AND WHO EXACTLY AM I?

Every day we encounter, again and again, adults with low self-esteem, which can give rise to many other issues, including an inferiority complex, that threaten our well-being and are unbearable for others to witness. It can also result in inflated self-worth and false self-esteem, which is just as intolerable for others.

SELF-CONFIDENCE:	SELF-WORTH:
Is when I have confidence in my own abilities – in what I can do.	Is when I think of myself as a valuable human being – who I am as a person.
Is inextricably linked to competencies.	Is inextricably linked to my identity.
High self-confidence gives me faith that I can do anything.	High self-worth gives me the belief that I am a valuable person who has value for myself and for others.
Low self-confidence tells me that I fail at anything that I throw myself into.	Low self-worth cast doubts on whether I have any value to others, and whether I deserve what I have achieved.

Poor self-esteem negatively affects confidence: "I don't matter, so what am I good for?" Similarly, good self-esteem positively affects confidence, creating a long-lasting confidence that does not fail when we meet resistance.

High self-esteem creates self-confidence, but self-confidence does not automatically create high self-esteem.

The question, therefore, of whether or not we want our children to have low or high self-esteem and self-confidence is rhetorical. As parents, there are two techniques we can utilise. However, if we use them unconsciously, there is a great risk that we will achieve the opposite of what we want. If, on the other hand, we use them consciously, then we cannot fail to be successful in our undertaking.

AIM:	AVOID:
To talk equally to everyone	Talking condescendingly to people
To be present	Taunting people
To show genuine interest	Ignoring people
To acknowledge people in speech and action	Speaking disparagingly of others' identity: "I do not like you when you ..."
To be honest and sincere	Using (adult-only) irony
To acknowledge actions	Praising actions
(Only if necessary) To criticize actions: "I do not like that you..."	Evaluating others

Our tools are what we say and what we do.

There is much we can say and do to strengthen our child's self-esteem and confidence, and as mentioned earlier, we don't need to worry about them not having confidence. In today's world, children get so much attention that they will probably gain plenty of confidence – unless we persistently criticise their actions.

The single biggest cause of low self-esteem in our children is, in fact, that we constantly applaud their actions. We need to stop this, and instead acknowledge them for being the person they are.

It is also worth noting that it is far easier to start this process if your own self-esteem is good. If you feel you are lacking in self-esteem, then start with yourself. As you increase your own self-esteem, it will rub off on your child, and vice versa: as you increase your child's self-esteem, it will surely rub off on you, so it is a win-win situation!

INTERNALLY DRIVEN OR EXTERNALLY CONTROLLED?

Many new parents' handbooks tell parents that children should have responsibilities according to what stage they are at in their development, and that too much responsibility too soon can create insecure children. Something that is less appreciated is what can happen if our children get responsibility too late, or don't get it at all.

When you assume responsibility for all of the functions in your child's life, they get so used to it that they automatically become externally-controlled instead of internally-driven. When we are externally-controlled, we hand over responsibility for what is good for us to others. When we are internally-driven, we accept and take responsibility for our own well-being ourselves.

Very young children are incapable of internally-driving themselves, and, therefore, it is a natural part of parenting to assume the role of external-control. Mothers, in particular, are assumed to know best when their children have to pee, are hungry, need to put warm clothes on or are sleepy, as well as a range of other basic needs – and, therefore, they assume a natural responsibility for the child. The challenge is recognising when the child is ready to take over responsibility for those same basic needs, so that as soon as possible the child can be internally-driven.

CONSTANTLY UNSURE OF THEIR CHOICES

An internally-driven child can feel and understand themselves and their needs, while an externally-controlled child does not feel or understand themselves because they have become accustomed to others taking that responsibility.

As parents, we, therefore, do our children a disservice by controlling them externally for too long, but we must also ensure that they do not crumble under all the responsibility.

The problem for the externally-controlled child arises the day they become a teenager and move out from the loving parental embrace. At that point, the teenager themselves must find out their own needs and how to deal with them, in addition to all the other things that young adults need to control.

As parents, we, therefore, do our children a disservice by controlling them externally for too long, but we must also ensure that they do not crumble under all the responsibility.

Not long ago, we worked with a young woman called Helle who was very, very confused. She was 20 years old and had just moved away from home and in with her boyfriend. Helle was distraught about what she should choose in life. She asked friends and family for advice and as everyone offered a different answer, she was constantly changing her mind and was deeply unsure whether or not her choice was the right one for her. When we met her, she was deeply depressed and felt inadequate in all areas of her life, despite the fact that she was very intelligent. Helle was about to give up.

But we had some ideas. Helle was strongly externally-controlled, with no experience in feeling what was right for her. After an intensive process where we worked on developing Helle's awareness and consciousness of her own needs and feelings, she was ready to go out into the world with a new – and secure – internal drive; a secure internal drive that she could have had since childhood.

As humans we thrive when we take responsibility for our own lives – and have it easiest when we don't!

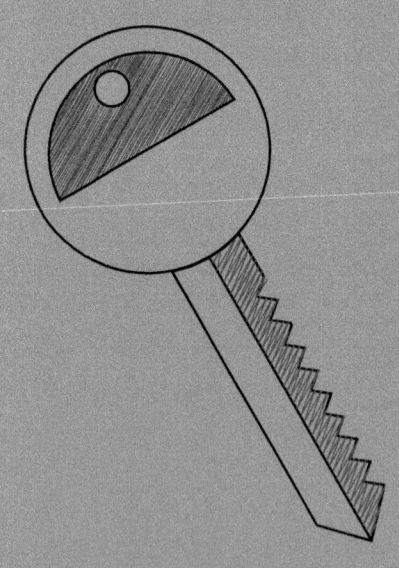

RESPONSIBILITY, OWNERSHIP AND TRUST

When Amelina was 13 months old, Mitzi and I removed her nappy in the belief that she would quickly figure out when she needed to do a number one or number two – and would act accordingly. We were inspired by a lively Finnish mother in our mothers' group who had done this with her four children.

Our friends with children aged 2 and 3 still in nappies thought we were mad. We did have a few weeks of running around with disinfectant and cloths, but that was it. Amelina learned quite quickly when she was going to do what, and went to the potty herself.

And like so many other parents, we had preconceptions about food: we had a lot of rules about how much Amelina had to eat, how and when. When Amelina was four years old, this resulted in a lot of arguments, tiresome mealtimes, a reluctance to eat and other gruelling situations that you may also have experienced.

At one of our monthly meetings, where Mitzi and I discuss whether what we do is good enough and appropriate for Amelina's stage in development, we discussed how we had ended up in this situation. We were, of course, both well aware that few children in Denmark die of hunger and that the public health nurse could not see any obvious signs of scurvy in our daughter.

"MAYBE I COULD DECIDE FOR MYSELF?"

The result was a radical decision. We arranged a meeting with Amelina, with the objective of making a new framework for eating. Amelina looked up sceptically from her jigsaw when we explained the idea to her, and clearly she expected the worst. It was a clear sign to us that it was high time we took the problem in hand.

At the meeting, which was very official, with juice and cinnamon swirls, we explained to Amelina that we didn't think it was going particularly well with mealtimes. We asked her what she thought we should do.

Amelina looked at us curiously, chewed her cinnamon swirl, and said, a little cautiously, 'Well, maybe I could decide myself, how much I should eat?'

Mitzi and I looked at each other and realised that Amelina didn't understand that we had expected some such reaction. However, we had a plan ready and decided there and then in partnership with Amelina that from now on she could decide herself whether or not she would eat and how much. We did, however, establish some ground rules: if Amelina didn't want to eat with us, she could then only decide between the same dish and rye bread when she was hungry.

THE LUNCHBOX

Another ground rule we established was that when Amelina ate with us, she had to try new foods. That way she could learn that something could taste good, even if it didn't look so appetising! Our final ground rule was a one-month trial period, where her responsibility could be revoked if we felt she was lacking in energy or nutrients to go to school, play or have fun.

We agreed on all the rules and the framework, and Project Responsibility for Taking Care of Ourselves was officially put in place for a radiant and visibly relieved Amelina, who immediately announced that she wanted to pack her own lunchbox.

From that day on, mealtimes were (and still are) a pleasure. Amelina always eats with us and from the outset has eaten more than she used to. She clearly enjoys the responsibility and there has been no more playing up since the project began.

WHEN AM I TIRED, DAD?

After a few months, Amelina came to us and asked how we thought it was going with mealtimes. We had to admit that it was going really well and she had shown that she had lived up to our trust.

'Could I be responsible for something else?' she asked, smiling.

'What did you have in mind?' I asked her, with an idea of the answer.

'I would like to be responsible for when I have to go to bed!' she said, exactly as I'd thought she might.

Mitzi and I looked hesitantly at each other, but agreed to participate in the meeting to which she invited us in the next breath.

We came to the meeting well-prepared, but Amelina did, too. She had all her arguments ready. Naturally, she used our own weapons against us, and informed us that we should believe it would work. We couldn't do anything but agree that our 5-year-old daughter should take over responsibility for bedtimes every day.

Our only requirement was that she be able to get up when we called her in the mornings without trouble, and that she would be fresh and able for school.

WHEN THE CLOCK NO LONGER DICTATES BEDTIME

We involved Amelina's surprised – but positive – teacher in the project, and agreed with her that if she felt that Amelina was tired or lethargic in school, then she would suggest going to bed earlier to her.

We reasoned that Amelina would probably stretch her new privileges to the fullest and be exhausted for a few days. But we also believed that it would even out naturally over time.

That didn't happen. She really took on the responsibility and asked to be informed of the time every half hour after eight o'clock, so she could navigate her new domain.

After three days, she sat on the floor of her room, at half past nine in the evening, a little upset.

'Dad, I can't figure out when I'm supposed to go to bed!" she said.

It was a quite reasonable and natural cry for help. Jørgen and Amelina had a chat about learning how to feel you that are tired, when you've been used to others knowing it better than yourself, and to the clock dictating bedtime.

The arrangement is permanent today, and Amelina is very happy about her privileges. We have made a number of amendments to our agreement: grown-up time after nine o'clock and no movies, games or bedtime stories then. It is a behavioural change, but still not a removal of Amelina's responsibility for her own bedtime. She is amazingly fresh all day despite her relatively late bedtime. We would not have discovered this had it been us who decided!

HOW MUCH RESPONSIBILITY IS YOUR CHILD READY FOR?

Today, Amelina has an extra sense that she frequently engages. She "feels" things, and that is a really good supplement to the more rational approach to life.

At some point in our lives, we decide, subconsciously, whether we will be rational-thinking type people, emotional-feeling type people, or a bit of both. The decision is about what we have become accustomed to, and the degree of success we have had with that choice. In our work, we have met many clients who have a preference for one type, but it provides only part of the picture.

Generally, we don't believe that it is better to feel than to think – or vice-versa. At the same time, we believe that a balance between the rational head and the emotional gut gives us useful additional information about the state of things, which makes it easier for us to make informed choices in life.

Another way to qualify our children to use both reason and emotion in their lives is by asking them for both.

For example:

"What do you think about going to see your grandmother for two days?"

"What is your gut telling you?"

***

Also, try to notice if your child uses the phrase "feels" and knows what it means.

How much responsibility is your child ready for – and how do you know?

A PERSON WHO FEELS THE WORLD

All children are different. We say that to each other quite often as parents. And although we are probably alike in more ways than we are different, there is a significant difference in our children, which is crucial for how they experience, perceive and, thereby, learn.

In fact, we are all either born with or acquire a system of representation. It is the sense we use the most, the sense that is our favourite. For some, it is such a clear-cut favourite that they practically can't "understand" the other senses, while others find it easier to use multiple representation systems.

WE HAVE A FAVOURITE SENSE

This system centres on how we experience things. We have five senses: namely, sight, hearing, touch, smell and taste. We are so ingeniously designed that we all have one or more favourites among these senses, a way we unconsciously prefer to experience things. It is often quite fundamental to what profession we end up in as adults.

Most of us are what we call visually-oriented; we experience things through pictures. This is reflected in the language we use, where we mainly use terms that are in tune with imagery. Those of us who are visually-oriented will often say things like: "I see" or "I imagine" or "You must see that...". The visual person tries to get an overview and is often hampered by disturbing visual impressions.

A smaller proportion of us are what we call auditory, experiencing the world through sound. They think best, for example, by talking to themselves – perhaps by moving their lips while doing so. Auditory

people can be distracted by sounds that others would not notice and will often express themselves with "sound" words and phrases such as: "It sounds like..." or "I can clearly hear that...". They often speak slowly while savouring the words and use "uh" and "hmmm" sounds while they think.

Yet another group is kinaesthetic, those of us who prefer to "feel" when we think, and often follow emotions and gut feelings. The kinaesthetic person will typically use "feeling" words such as: "It's tangible" ,"I am standing by it" and "You can understand...". The kinaesthetic appreciates physical contact. They will often lay a hand on someone's shoulder and will often stand closer to other people than other types. They can physically feel if things feel right.

The two remaining groups are olfactory and gustatory; their dominant senses are smell and taste respectively.

INCREASE YOUR IMPACT

But why is it important to know this in relation to our children? It is important to know for many reasons. Firstly, our representation system is essential to and for our learning. Secondly, we can easily increase our impact by knowing our children's "language" and speaking it with the child. Thirdly, we can quite effortlessly teach our children to "understand several languages" (e.g., body language). This helps to avoid conflict, particularly if different languages are "spoken" by the children and the parents, as without understanding why, they endure frustrating situations, simply because they do not understand each other.

BE IN SYNC

Some time ago, Jørgen was at a party and fell into conversation with a music producer, who obviously favoured the auditory system of representation without knowing it. He shared his biggest problem with Jørgen: he and his sister could not communicate about their elderly parents. Shaking his head, he told Jørgen that he had asked his sister whether "they could speak as one to their parents" and she had replied that she "could not feel where he was" in relation to them.

"It's weird that she says she can't feel me when I was talking about needing to be in sync," he said, clearly frustrated.

Clearly the problem was one of different languages: they simply did not understand each other.

Schools rarely take into account a child's favourite representation system, because teachers – despite learning about the different re-presentational systems – do not examine their own, and so reflexively communicate based on their own representation system. A visual teacher who speaks in pictures does not have the same understanding with the auditory learner as they do with the visual learner.

If we look briefly at the learning conditions for the three most common representation systems, then we can say that the visual people learn best by reading, watching demonstrations, looking at the board and creating reminders. The auditory group learns best by hearing instructions and stories told in quiet surroundings. Kinaesthetic children are very action-oriented, and learn best by trying things out; for example, learning their times tables through playing hopscotch.

CRACK YOUR CHILDS LANGUAGE CODE

As a parent, you have the opportunity to discover your child's favourite representation system and to use that to communicate. It requires you knowing your own preferred representation system, so you know whether your system is different from your child's. It means that you must be rather good at learning how to communicate in your child's terms instead of your own, using the linguistic metaphors that belong to your child's preffered representation system.

This calls for increased awareness in everyday life, maybe you can get help from either your child or your partner? Once you've cracked the code, you will find that your child will suddenly pay more attention to what you say, and you will avoid many cases of getting your wires crossed, when you talk to each other.

It is perhaps worth remembering that most of us are capable of perceiving and understanding with more than one representation system, and, therefore, our children learn a lot, regardless of how teachers choose to speak to them. But just think how much more they could learn if we spoke a "language" that they fully understood.

A good exercise is to start listening to the language patterns that you hear around you.
You will find yourself, relatively quickly, decoding the representation systems around you that you prefer.

What is your child's favourite sense?
And what is your own?

FUNDAMENTAL PARENTAL STRATEGIES

As parents, we have a fundamental choice – the choice of parental strategy. It could also be a choice not to have any parental strategy. Here, all decisions are ad hoc and perhaps, therefore, have no consistency or predictability.

We don't need to judge whether or not the impact of a particular strategy is important. However, we have a suspicion that you, as a parent, work a lot of overtime as you have to continuously invent the ground-rules, instead of having a set of rules that give space to and allow for most of what you encounter in parenting.

A clear parental strategy will be very beneficial in the long run. Many of the things we as adults have a particular opinion about – regardless of whether we appreciate or despise them – are quite often strikingly consistent with how we saw them as children.

A clear parental strategy will be very beneficial in the long run. 🙶

One way to create a strategy – and also to update it in line with the child's developing needs and abilities – is to keep checking in on the status of your parenting with each other as parents.

GO WITH THE FLOW

Jørgen and I have, over the years, held various meetings at home where we sit down and discuss specific challenges and put together a strategy. Sometimes these meetings are with Amelina; those we call family meetings. Other times, it is just us.

Many people have regular morning meetings at work – perhaps once a week or once a month, where the current status and strategies are looked at and drawn up for the future. But in perhaps the 'most important task of our lives, giving our children the best conditions to grow and develop, many of us end up just going with the flow. We do not take the time to reflect on what we are doing and why we are doing it. In many aspects of life, we believe that it makes sense to leave something to chance; to trust in the process and not control everything. But in relation to our children, it really does pay off to consciously consider whether what we do is good enough – or whether or not it is time to do something else.

We have made it a habit to meet over a cup of coffee in the evening, especially if one of us has a feeling that something is happening with Amelina which requires a special focus. Children develop almost from week to week, which is why we as parents also need to develop a way to help everyone involved deal with this. Otherwise, a mismatch will slowly evolve.

It's nice to see it coming, and that way, we can avoid having to one day ask our grown-up children if they have remembered to wash their hands before dinner!

As parents, we are the victims of habitual thinking.

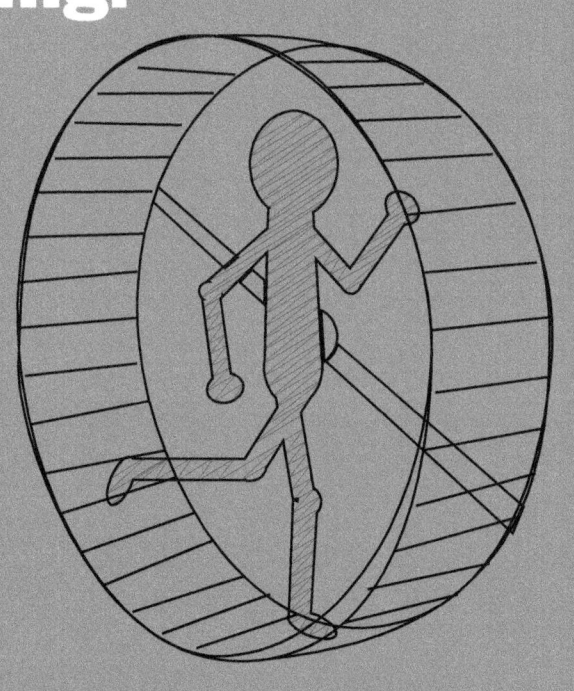

PLACE FOR DISAGREEMENT

As parents, we are the victims of habitual thinking. We don't think about what we usually do, and if we don't think about what we usually do, then we just do what we usually do – even if some other action or reaction would be a far better response.

At the meetings, Jørgen and I decide our parental strategy after we have discussed the current challenges and the possible ways of dealing with them.

We also ask ourselves whether what we are doing at that moment is the best option for the situation, and we discuss – sometimes quite passionately – the right course of action. Of course, we do not agree on everything, but the most important thing is that we make decisions which we can both endorse. Otherwise, our statements in everyday life result in confusion and insecurity – and give Amelina an opportunity to play us off against each other.

One decision we constantly discuss, and which we do not yet fully agree on, is whether Amelina has complete responsibility for her bedtime. In practice, she has full responsibility, but I, Mitzi, believe that there should be an upper limit, while Jørgen believes that that is the equivalent of depriving Amelina of responsibility, which is what it's all about. He argues that it is unnecessary because Amelina never goes to bed after ten o'clock on weekdays. She goes to bed when she is tired.

Practical questions can easily reach ideological heights, resulting in children who are not fully aware of which rules apply in particular situations – even when they try to navigate things as best they can.

By holding regular meetings, you have a place to discuss questions, issues, events and challenges and so on, including those things that you have different attitudes to – instead of discussing them over the heads of your children.

> **What changes do you think such meetings could create in your daily life?**

OWNERSHIP

Ownership of one's own life is one of the most basic factors that motivates most people.

At work, you've probably experienced being able to realise a good idea; it feels much better and is more motivating than realising other people's ideas.

It is exactly the same in daily life. A playhouse that we have built ourselves, will give us greater pleasure than the one we bought in a shop – just like when children get to pick what's for dinner and are allowed to help make it. It tastes much better to them than the meal that is "just" standing on the table.

> *Ownership of one's own life is one of the most basic factors that motivates most people.*

Once we have ownership of successful projects, then we have a stake in them, and that is important for motivation, self-esteem, pride and joy.

There is an exciting challenge in ensuring that our children receive the best opportunities for ownership of their lives and their projects, especially because we may well feel that we 'own' them slightly and thus want "a stake" in their lives and projects.

THROW OUT THE TRAINING WHEELS

When we teach developmental processes, we use a metaphor about a child learning to ride a bike in order to explain the diffe-rence between a counsellor, a mentor, a coach and an *EmpowerMind Trainer*.

While the counsellor explains how to cycle, and the mentor de-monstrates it, the *EmpowerMind Trainer* or coach will run alongside the bike and support the child mentally, allowing the child to learn from their mistakes in the process. The main purpose of this is to get the child to acquire full ownership of the process of learning to ride a bike. It is motivational, gives them responsibility, and boosts their self-esteem and confidence.

We experienced exactly this on the day that Amelina learned to ride a bike without training wheels. Over the years, Jørgen had seen plenty of fathers, dripping with sweat, as they chased their children's bicycles with a hand firmly anchored on the stabilising stick.

Now it was time for him to "walk-the-talk"; for a hand on the stick would, of course, be the same as taking responsibility away from Amelina.

PERSONAL PROTECTIVE ARMOUR

One beautiful spring morning, when the sun shone over the treetops, Jørgen and Amelina went down to a nearby park, which would, at least, ensure a soft landing.

Amelina wore personal protective armour for safety. Out on the park's grass, Jørgen invited her, with well-hidden nervousness, to go for a spin on her bike.

Amelina looked at him momentarily from under the bicycle helmet's rim, judging the situation, and set off over the lawn. It didn't look 100% stable, but for a while it went really well, and Amelina cycled further and further away while Jørgen was glued to the lawn. Suddenly, something happened, and Amelina flew over the handlebars and landed in a heap in the middle of the football field.

With misgivings, Jørgen ran out to the scene and asked a dazed but otherwise unharmed little girl what had happened.

"I fell, Dad!" Amelina said, irritated at being asked to state the obvious – did the old man get a knock on the head, too?!

Jørgen gathered all the confidence he could possibly muster, and asked, hopefully: "What did you do that made you fall?"

This time, Amelina thought long and hard before she answered: "I was looking for you, and then I turned the handlebars, and then I fell."

"Okay," he replied, relieved, and added: "So, what should you do differently now?" Amelina thought again and replied: "I shouldn't turn the handlebars."

"So, when you are not turning the handlebars, what do you do instead?" he asked, much more comfortable now.

Amelina replied promptly: "Well, I keep the handlebars even and look straight ahead."

IT'S WORKING!

And so off she went again with a clear strategy, feeling a bit more sure of herself. A few more instructive crashes later, and it was time to go home, this time cycling on the somewhat harder pavement.

Amelina was exhilarated when she greeted Mitzi in front of the house: "Mum, mum, I've learned to ride a bike all by myself," she shouted, just about to fall over.

We are quite sure that all children are proud when they learn to cycle, but, at the same time, we could feel Amelina beam with a fundamental pride that she had 100% ownership of her own project.

Jørgen had just mentally "run along beside her" and supported her.

DO WHAT WE SAY

When there is consistency between our words, expressions and actions, we are congruent. That means that we do what we say – and we say what we do, and we say what we mean – and mean what we say.

Many people find it difficult to deal with people who say they will do something, but do something else or nothing at all. We are confused by it, or see it as hypocrisy. We get distracted and unsettled if we have a sense that the other person is saying something they don't really mean.

Many people find it difficult to deal with **"**
people who say they will do something, but
do something else or nothing at all.

It is the same for children, and they are perhaps even better able to intuitively decode when adults are being congruent.

A few weeks ago, we were visiting some friends who have some lovely but unruly children. At one point, the father complained that his daughter never does what he says. His daughter overheard this.

Mitzi chose to share an observation with the father, one that she has often encountered in other contexts. She explained that she had observed that when the father said something serious, something he really meant, to his daughter, he didn't look like he meant it, for the simple reason that he always said it with a smile. It sounds like such a little thing, and perhaps it is, but it does not change its significance.

Every dog owner knows that if you want your dog to obey, you have to mean what you say, as dogs decode not only the spoken word, but equally the tone and the unspoken elements. And without comparing our children to dogs, children do exactly the same – regardless of age.

DON'T PLAY GUESSING GAMES WITH THE MESSAGE

Therefore, the congruence between the message and body language is crucial to the success of the message. The father started to believe what he was saying, and it was not long before his daughter often did what he asked.

Maybe you say serious things to your child in a smiling, friendly and mild manner to protect your child from verbal abuse, and that is commendable. Or maybe you have a hard time making demands on your child – or believing that your child will do what you say?

Your child does not come to harm from you being certain in your communication. It is far more harmful to the child if they can't understand what you really mean. In this situation, the child will have to guess at what you mean, and they have a lot of potential for guessing wrong, and thus being scolded by a parent who has been emotionally hijacked by abandonment and frustration.

A breach of trust between adults happens easily when one party does not live up to or fails to fulfil the agreement. We might let it pass once, possibly a few more times if it is a family member or a friend who has breached our trust. Our children accept our many, many breaches of trust because they love us, but it is harmful for both our relationship with them and especially for the child's own perception of what is acceptable.

If you can allow yourself to break agreements with your child, then your child receives permission for exactly the same behaviour later in life. It can come to cost them dearly in friendships and their career.

In the name of congruence, here are two questions to reflect on:

What causes you to break agreements you have made?
How can you prevent yourself entering into such agreements?

You may want to include your answers to these questions in your parental strategy, so your partner or spouse can help to ensure that you stick to the strategy.

Another facet of congruence is what we call "walking-the-talk": doing what we say we will do. You've probably heard the statement, "Your child does not what you say, but what you do". This means, for example, that if you say that we should not use bad language, but then you do it, you have automatically cancelled the message. It may sound obvious, but it must be noted, as this principle also applies to the more subtle subconscious plane, which is slightly trickier.

Your child chooses childish strategies, a bit like you choosing parental strategies, but with a difference: your child will typically choose one of two strategies. If your strategy is positive, the child will typically choose the same strategy as you, whereas if your strategy is negative, your child will typically choose the same – or the opposite.

AN ALLERGY TO NEGATIVITY

Thus, if you have chosen to spend a lot of your time sulking about and nit-picking your surroundings, there is an imminent risk that your child will choose the same negative behaviour in relation to their surroundings. But, fortunately, there is also a chance that your child, in spite of your behaviour, will choose the opposite: to be happy and generous. The child will likely then have an "allergy" to sulking and to nit-picking.

However, if you choose the positive approach, you have the chance to win big. Which unconscious strategy you have in play is uncertain, as it can often be dictated by unconscious emotional hijacking. But, fortunately, our children are the mirror in which we can look and find out!

Not long ago, we were quite annoyed with Amelina because she continually said that everything was annoying – often accompanied by a slight sigh. We asked her repeatedly to stop, which was obviously not helpful. Only when we took a step back and reflected on the situation did we find out that it was probably due to both us having the same bad habit without being aware of it.

Now we had the opportunity to support each other in finding another habit, and we knew that we no longer needed to articulate Amelina's statements. That would probably happen all by itself, when we ourselves changed strategy.

What bad habits and characteristics does your child have? What does your child do that annoys you?

In the answer, you might find the key to your own behaviour and strategies, which can help both yourself and your child.

" "

Showing your child trust is one of the strongest tools you can use to strengthen your child's self-worth.

TRUST

We believe that trust is one of the basic human characteristics, and it is crucial for quality in our relationships. At the same time, trust is one of the properties that is most exposed to being attacked in life.

When a child is born, they have unlimited confidence that the world is good. When one of our friends had his child baptised, the pastor said something that hit the mark: "When the baby cries, really he is asking a question. He is asking if the world is good. The answer depends on whether you come and comfort your child or not!"

Every time we as humans experience failures, big and small, we unconsciously – but surely – change our approach to the concept of trust. Slowly, we start to learn from our failures, and we may choose distrust rather than confidence; distrust of the world around us and the people we associate with, distrust of our colleagues, family and, perhaps also, our child.

So the first time your child does not live up to your trust, you respond with disenchantment, following an unconscious logic: "Well, there's one more person, I can't trust."

TRUST IS POWERFUL

When we are met with distrust, we can feel it. It makes us feel inferior, anxious, worried and unsure of ourselves. This is also the case for your child.

If this has not happened yet, then it almost certainly will happen: one day, your child will not live up to your (possibly) high demands, and it will be easy to – unconsciously – respond with distrust.

However, you have a choice, and that is to continue to show your children unlimited trust despite being disappointed by them not living up to your expectations. Disappointments are indeed related to your standards and your worldview, and perhaps your child is in the process of developing their own standards and worldview.

Showing your child trust is one of the strongest tools you can use to strengthen your child's self-worth. We can sense when someone shows us great trust. It warms our insides on the coldest of days.

From when Amelina was quite young, she liked to go exploring on her own in the shops we went into. Initially, we thought of everything terrible that could happen to her, but, on the other hand, we had not read very often about children who disappeared in stores. Therefore, quite early on, we gave Amelina permission to explore shops. We only had one clear rule: "You must stay in the shop!" (Rather than "You must not go out of the shop.")

We can all decide for ourselves if we will show "" *not just our children, but the world around us, trust or distrust.*

In the beginning, we took turns to keep a discreet eye on Amelina, but she was too busy exploring all the aisles of the shop. We soon saw that she lived up to our trust. It was a mutual agreement and we all stayed in the shop until we were all ready to leave it. Amelina was not yet four years old but we let her loose in shops all over the world!

Amelina knows deep in her heart that in doing this, we have placed a very, very high level of trust in her, and she has never abused it.

If we choose to show the world distrust, there is a great chance that we will be disappointed again and again and, therefore, will continue to choose distrust. Here, we believe in the worst and so that is what we experience in the world.

If, on the other hand, we choose to show the world trust, then we may only be disappointed once in a while, as we believe the best and so are pleasantly surprised. As we have mentioned before: we get what we focus on!

This also applies to our children.

NOT TOO MUCH EGO-TRIPPING

As we wrote at the beginning of this book, we often think of our children as projects; projects with an impending danger of becoming egocentric, ruthless and attention-seeking:

♦ The more attention our children get, the more addictive it becomes.

♦ The more we pamper our children, the more they demand.

♦ The more exaggerated a focus their needs get, the more ruthless they become.

♦ The more self-confident the children are, the more egocentric and self-obsessed they become.

♦ The more we remove our children's problems, the more fragile they become.

In other words, although we, with the best of intentions, give our children the best that we can and have, it may lead to them developing into unbearably selfish and ruthless children and young people, who no one can cope with.

Therefore, focus, attention, generosity and good intentions need to be balanced by something which ensures that our children also develop some of the crucial social skills that make it both easier for themselves and for others to deal with them now and in the future.

It is in fact their brain development that causes children to be preoccupied with themselves and their own needs – often right up to their 20s. Any behaviour that deviates from this rule is learned, and not an expression of natural behaviour.

Fortunately, it is not difficult to learn different behaviour. It requires an awareness and congruence with their parents – and then just persistent work! The counterweight to all the unpleasant things we have listed above is a cocktail of the ingredients listed below.

Demands

We put demands on our children: small chores for which they receive a little reward. They discover that few things in life – except love – are "free" and that if they demand something of us, then we demand something of them.

Consequences

In daily life, we strive to stick to our decisions until we find out that they are wrong – and then we stick to the new decisions.

Change of Perspective

In situations where children (naturally) only see things from their perspective, we help them to see things from the other's perspective, to allow them to experience the situation from a different perspective than their own.

A Holistic View

We try our best to balance how we deal with our children, so they are not only treated as individuals, but also as part of a group, e.g., in kindergarten or at a party.

Overcoming Challenges

Here, we as parents have a difficult challenge, because it hurts us when our children suffer. We will not solve their conflicts and problems for them, but we will go to extremes to help them solve them. There is a tremendous difference between the two approaches, and the consequences are self-esteem, pride, ownership and resilience.

Respecting other's needs

Children believe that their needs are the most important. That is not so strange given that many adults do, too. We have a strong focus on our needs and believe that they are as important as our children's. It is about adult-time, not having to play when we do not want to play, having peace to read the newspaper, children not interrupting us when we or other adults are talking, and children knowing and applying ordinary social rules, such as greeting people and saying thank you for food.

Self-worth
We believe that by us doing our utmost to build our children's self-esteem, they can relax so much in themselves that they have more energy for others.

Walking-the-talk
Our behaviour as parents is the crucial factor in our children's behaviour. If we as parents are selfish or exclude others, then there is a very high possibility that our children will be just like us. The more respect we as parents show each other and others, and the better we talk about others when they are not present, the more likely it is that our children will develop the same inclusive and social competences.

HANDLE CONFLICTS IN A GOOD WAY

Do you know how it feels to be checkmated by a six year old? Our children often emotionally hijack us during conflicts with them – despite us know-it-all adults working so hard to get the last word in!

But what exactly is the children's positive intention for boycotting vegetables, wearing a tulle skirt in winter or consistently coming to the dinner table ten minutes after you have called them?

We believe that some conflicts are good, because they help children develop and create new ways of thinking – especially when they have to pick themselves up again! However, many conflicts are unnecessary, draining the positive energy and sense of community from the family. You can easily eradicate them from your life.

Here, you can read what being truly and completely present can achieve.

THE DRAMA TRIANGLE

One of the most wasteful and unhealthy dynamics that can sneak into a family, and other relationships that you or your child are part of, is "The Drama Triangle".

The drama triangle is so-called because it is a drama that unfolds when there are three participants, even if only two are performing.

Let us be clear; it is not certain that you are involved in a drama triangle right now, but it is quite likely that at some point you were, and that you will be again.

Some people live their entire lives in drama triangles, while others just participate as guests.

WHAT DO YOU DO?

If you are involved in a triangle, then it is quite likely that your child is also. The triangles in which we participate as children are the ones that can have the most negative impact on our lives as adults.

A drama triangle has the following players: the victim, the rescuer and the persecutor

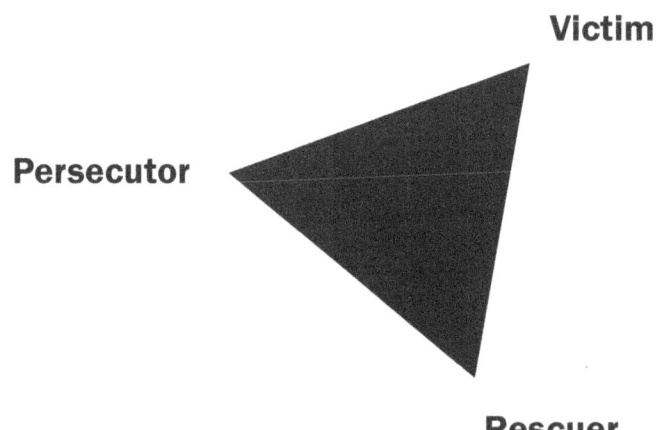

THE VICTIM

Characteristic to the victim is that everything is the fault of others. The victim blames negative things in their own life on anyone other than themselves: their parents, their partner, the neighbour or the government. They don't take any responsibility for their own life; rather, they believe that as others have put them in a hopeless situation, only that "other" has the power to release them from said situation. However, if someone manages to gets them out of a hopeless situation, another external cause comes to the fore instead, again allowing them to avoid taking responsibility.

The victim is typically recognised by statements such as: "I can't develop myself because of my boss", "She doesn't understand me", "I can't...myself", "It's not my fault", "With this government I'll never get a job" and "I have to do everything myself".

THE RESCUER

Rescuers see it as their primary duty to save everyone around them. At first, this sounds sympathetic, but they do it – unconsciously – to win acknowledgment from others. They seek the feeling of success. Acknowledgement from others is their fuel, and, therefore, they live their lives based on others, instead of taking care of their own needs. They feed on the nutrients that are in acknowledgment. Rescuers are, therefore, very externally-controlled. Other peoples' opinions of them are far more important than what they think about themselves.

"Fortunately", there are lots of victims crying for help, so rescuers are often found working in social and health care services, or as some kind of therapist. Rescuers are so adept at becoming involved in and accepting others' problems that they can avoid dealing with their own issues. You often hear rescuers making compassionate statements such as: "It's hard for you", "I'm just trying to help", "I'll do it" and "Let me fix that for you".

However, it is not just in the care sector that rescuers are found. They are found in many other workplaces and in everyday life as well.

THE PERSECUTOR

Persecutors are a little more complex, because they can take two guises: one negative, and one which at first seems positive. In the negative guise, they are often bitter and irritated with others, because, for example, the others have not lived up to their expectations. Persecutors are recognised by statements such as: "If you want something done right, you have to do it yourself!", "You just have to get up to speed now!", "It's just not good enough!" and "You haven't put your plate in the dishwasher again!"

In the seemingly positive guise, a persecutor may be experienced as a more positive force, but they use guilt as a very effective wea-pon for maintaining their position of power over others. They can, for example, say things like: "How can you say that when you know how much I'm hurting?" and "All I wanted was a nice, quiet evening".

In the extreme, persecutors abuse their spouses. You may have heard others say "But he's just a poor thing himself", and that is exactly what he is.

A VICTIM RADAR

We all have a preferred role for the drama triangles in which we participate, and we "visit" them according to how often we participate in a drama triangle: some only rarely but others more frequently, as they live most of their lives in a drama triangle.

Actually, all three roles are victims, just with a different expression. They are victims of themselves – and of each other.

A very strong mutual attraction exists that allows rescuers to easily find victims, for they are found everywhere, and they cry for help. And those cries for help are clear to anyone with a radar for victims. The victim is also very good at spotting a rescuer, and so the relationship is set in play.

The rescuer can easily perceive a persecutor as a victim, and is indeed often the only one who can do so, and they love (trying to) save them, despite the fact that they repeatedly receive verbal or physical abuse for their efforts. Persecutors love chastising both rescuers

All three rolls are victims, just with a different expression. They are victims of themselves – and of each other.

and victims, as they live up nicely to the persecutor's own feeling of inadequacy.

Thus, the drama is well and truly alive, and if one of the parties disappears, a new one replaces them almost immediately.

THE ROLLS CHANGE AROUND AS NEEDED

The three roles are incredibly interdependent and far from static. They can be reversed at will: for example, a persecutor can switch between the role of persecuting and being the victim: "Sorry, honey, I didn't mean it. My job is just making me so depressed."

In fact, we move frequently around the triangle, depending on which relationship we are in or what is happening in our lives. When we go through a life crisis, it is easy to become a victim. And when others we care about are ill, it often brings out the rescuer in us.

The major problem with drama triangles is that they beget unhealthy and inappropriate relationships of mutual dependence in such a way that we retain certain roles that we inhabit again and again, if and when we return to the same, or a similar, drama triangle.

When the rescuer saves a victim by saying: "That's a pity for you, let me...", the rescuer is doing the direct opposite of what is appropriate. They enable the victim to remain in the role of victim, instead of supporting the victim in taking responsibility for their own lives. The rescuer cannot risk doing this, since they would then lose their victim, and that is never appropriate in the drama triangle's unhealthy logic.

What role do you see yourself in most often?

CHILDREN IN THE DRAMA TRIANGLE

But why should we address the drama triangle in relation to our children? We should address it because children are inadvertently drawn into the drama triangles of their unaware parents (and others), and thus develop inappropriate behaviour, which can permeate their relationships and may radically limit them later in life.

In decidedly dysfunctional families where, for instance, the mother is suffering from alcoholism and from a very young age, the child has to take responsibility for both their mother and the younger siblings, it is almost predetermined that the child will enter the caring profession later in life. The child will be co-dependent, with limited or no contact with their own feelings and needs, a condition which will require therapy to reconcile.

It is not a prerequisite that a family be dysfunctional in order to establish drama triangles. In fact, most parents have one or more drama triangles in play at different times during the child's upbringing.

Imagine a father who is unemployed. He develops a victim mentality. The mother acquires the role of rescuer, but shifts gradually to the role of persecutor. The child must choose sides and becomes the father's rescuer. Eventually, the father returns to employment, perhaps relinquishing his victim role. The child, however, retains their "safe" rescuer mentality, never learning how to deal with or manage things themselves.

A CHILDHOOD ON THE SIDELINES

Another instance is the "behave yourself" family. Here, demands of high standards of accuracy and perfection are made. The child is severely reprimanded by the persecutor-mother and perhaps also by the father when they do something "wrong". The child quickly chooses a safe life as a victim on the sidelines; they can "never do anything right". It is the direct opposite of the parents' intention. Or, as a rescuer, the child does everything to please the strict parents and so becomes externally-controlled. They become so externally-controlled that as an adult, they do not know who they really are – and what really gives them value.

Similarly, a rescuer-mother who removes all obstacles for her ideal-child, with the best of intentions, makes the child lack responsibility for their own lives to such an extent that they grow up and become a dependent victim who always blames others for their misfortune. This was almost certainly not the good intentions which motivated the mother's actions.

Children are undeniably kept within drama triangles as parents (and others) continuously rescue them from all obstacles in life (which, in turn, causes the child to feel guilty), as well as drawing them into conflicts between the parents and overly criticising them.

If you recognise yourself as partaking in a drama triangle, it is pointless asking whether or not your child is also doing so. Quite simply: they are!

You have undoubtedly participated in drama triangles, albeit unconsciously. Now the only question remaining is for how long you will continue to do so. The choice is yours!

If you recognize yourself as partaking in a drama triangle, it is pointless asking whether or not your child is also doing so. Quite simply: they are!

OUT FROM THE TRIANGLE'S SHADOW

Fortunately, breaking out of drama triangles is achieved with a very straightforward method. It is a simple four-step process and you've already reached step two! There are, however, almost always some complications.

Step 1: is about understanding the existence and nature of drama triangles. This is a prerequisite for resolving your unconscious participation in a triangle.

Step 2: is about increasing your awareness of the triangles around you. We envisage that having completed step 1, it will be relatively easy for you to identify triangles in some of the relationships around you. The day you no longer see them is a clear indication that you have lost awareness of them. Therefore, you will have to return to this step. Your consciousness can help you to identify those triangles in which you participate, thereby, completing step two.

Step 3: is about consciously deciding to do something about the situation. A decision has consequences. This is where the process can become complicated. When you consciously decide to withdraw from a drama triangle, it is a decision that in one stroke can change a behaviour you have had since you were drawn into a particular drama triangle in childhood. It can mean confrontation or a showdown in close relationships. It may also require that you focus fully on your new behaviour until you are comfortable in your new role outside the triangle. This may mean confronting aspects of what "you believe" (e.g., "I'm just helping my child!").

Are you ready to make that decision?

132

Step 4: is about stepping out from the triangle's shadow. It is by far the easiest step. Stepping out means doing the opposite of what is expected or predicted of you in that situation. The trick then is to stay out of the triangle, despite triangle logic dictating that the remaining players, unconsciously, do everything in their power to draw you back into the triangle. It can be challenging, for they are people you love. The victim will unconsciously call for more scolding from the persecutor, or suddenly feel bad for calling the rescuer back. The persecutors will alternate between using guilt and threats to get the victim and rescuer back.

FORTUNATELY CHILDREN NATURALLY RESIST DRAMA TRIANGLES

A common drama triangle scenario is an adult-daughter breaking out of the rescuer role in relation to her elderly mother, who, in return, cashes in a lifetime's savings of "weapons". She presses all the right buttons – and may even threaten suicide to get her daughter back "on track".

That is how strong the drama triangle dynamics are!

Indeed, it is vital that we continuously check whether our children, albeit unconsciously, enter into such triangles around them, whether with the rest of your family, friends or teachers. Or even you!

Fortunately, children tend to naturally resist participation in drama triangles until their resistance is overcome by a superior force. Here, it is essential that we discern whether our children are thriving as they should be, and discuss the situation with them.

The simplest method of discerning this is by listening for signs of "triangle-role-talk" when the child speaks in your company or the company of others. Statements similar to:

"It's not my fault. It's the others!" – Victim
"She never does what I say!", "He is so stupid!" – Persecutor

Paying excessive attention to others and what others think are early rescuer characteristics.

You will likely hear some linguistic signs of triangle behaviour from your child every day. It is quite natural as children learn how to navigate their emotions. Only when there is a clear preference towards a particular way of communication is it appropriate to engage or challenge the statements. One way you can do this is with reframing (see p. 35).

WHEN YOU ARE HIJACKED BY YOUR EMOTIONS

The automatic emotional reaction is exactly that: automatic, and therefore, not easy to control. The point is that the automatic-feeling in itself only lasts a few seconds – some researchers say just six seconds! Thereafter, it is you who chooses to remain in that feeling, or replace it with one more beneficial.

When we "choose" to stay in an emotion, we quite often mean that we have become emotionally hijacked. Emotional hijacking is a static state, which is only beneficial for us if we are hijacked by a good emotion, such as falling in love. In negative emotional hijacking, we can lose access to our rationality. You might have experienced saying something you regretted afterwards – even to your children.

Emotional hijacking requires two actors, each bearing an equal responsibility for the hijacking: namely, the one doing the hijacking, and the one being hijacked.

Maybe you have a friend, a partner or a child who is really good at saying or doing things that make you fly into a rage. What they are doing is hijacking! On the other hand, there is another party who must authorise the hijacking. That's you!

Emotional hijacking requires two actors, who each bear an equal responsibility for the hijacking – namely, the one doing the hijacking, and the one being hijacked.

Indeed, no matter how much you desire it, you do not have a decisive influence on what other people say or do. You cannot change people. However, you do have crucial influence on how hijacked you want to be by their behaviour.

PRIORITIZING ENERGY SOURCES

Being emotionally hijacked by our children is a major threat to increasing our awareness of what is most appropriate for our children. It causes us to lose energy, overview, common sense and awareness, and with them, the opportunity for reconciliation.

It is easy to talk about energy, but to actually have it in abundance in everyday life in a family with small children is quite difficult. No doubt the parents of three small children who have not slept properly in two years believe, and hope, that energy is something that will return to them when the children have grown older. But this is a dangerous pretext, because energy is essential for success in parenting. None of the techniques and methods described in this book are easily accessible if you do not have the energy to focus on your own consciousness as a parent.

The key is prioritising what gives you the most energy: a sticky floor or happy, creative children making memories – and friends can always help cook when they come over for dinner.

Look at what time you spend on non-important things.
What could you spend your time on instead?

YOUR OWN PRIVATE OBSERVER

We are particularly susceptible to emotional hijacking when we are tired, and, therefore, being well-rested is necessary in relation to the mental development of your children.

However, it is not a natural law that we are more susceptible to emotional hijacking when we are tired. Rather our tired state requires us to place a greater focus on the desired emotion. Moreover, it is during our tired state that opportunities to practice emotional control come in abundance. And once we have mastered that, we no longer sweat the small stuff!

Both you and your child can practice emotional control with this little exercise: imagine a small version of yourself out on your shoulder. They are your own private observer. Next time you are emotionally hijacked, it is your observer's task to examine what emotional state you are in, and to question if that is the feeling you want. After a little practice, you can then choose the emotion that most benefits you.

CONFLICTS

An issue we are often asked about when giving talks or facilitating workshops on *EmpowerMind Training* for children, is how to handle conflicts. Conflict is an issue that concerns many parents, as it can hinder a good relationship and impede harmony in the home.

Obviously, there is no one solution to avoiding and resolving conflict, as all conflicts are inherently unique. Rather, here we offer some general considerations, which might help you resolve conflicts between you and your child or between your children.

We have a worldview that we believe is true, otherwise we would have chosen another one.

First and foremost, it is important to point out that it is not the conflict itself that is the problem, but the way we handle conflict. We have a tendency to see conflict as something negative, and that is something we would like to challenge. Conflicts arise when there are different expectations for a situation or different opinions about an issue.

In reality, this means that we each approach a conflict issue or si-tuation from the starting point of our worldview. That is what conflict is really about! And of course it is – where else, other than with our own worldview, would we start? We have a worldview that we believe is true, otherwise we would have chosen another one.

However, others rarely have the same worldview as us, but they naturally experience their world to be just as true as you experience your world – otherwise they would have chosen another one, too.

WHEN TWO WORLDS COLLIDE

It is quite natural that when two "truths" about the world meet, sparks are emitted. Actually it is a positive thing, because it is precisely through conflicts – confrontations with other worldviews – that we develop as humans.

If our worldview is never conflicted, then our "truth" becomes self-endorsed: we confirm that our worldview is the truth, and so we do not develop. Conflicts are, therefore, crucial for our development as human beings.

Essential questions here are:

> **Do you want your child to become a clone of yourself with the same worldview that you have built up through your life…?**
>
> **Or do you want your child to be an independent individual who builds their own worldview from their own and others' experiences?**

If you choose the former, then enter conflicts with the aim of winning, as every victory will increase the cloning potential – unless your child, at some point, chooses to rebel against this.

However, if you choose the latter, then conflicts are unique opportunities where both parties can debate their worldviews. If you choose to listen to each other, you may both become wiser. Imagine if your child was empowered to tell you that sometimes you are unreasonable or that you do not always have a patent on the right solution.

The risk with any conflict is that the participants can become emotionally hijacked and so do not act appropriately. It is not a given that your child would let themselves be hijacked, as it is not certain that you have taught your child how to choose their feelings yet. Furthermore, the child's "trying" of the various emotions and their consequences is vital for their navigation in life, and it is questionable whether it is appropriate for your young child to learn to restrain their emotions so quickly.

CHILDREN PUSH OUR BOUNDARIES TO THEIR LIMIT

You are not in the same situation as your child. Fortunately, you now know how to handle emotional hijacking, so if a conflict does escalate between you and your child, you can recognise it as feedback that you have let yourself be hijacked, despite your new knowledge. Feedback such as this is a great opportunity for training your consciousness to select the appropriate emotions.

Indeed, children are undoubtedly persistent players, so what better training partners could you wish for?

Generally, conflicts can be categorised as resulting from the following:

1. Different worldviews

2. Our children challenging our limits

3. Inappropriate parental behaviour

If you see your child as constantly pushing boundaries, it may be due to the boundaries being unclear. Or, in other words, your child doubts the position of the corner flags on their playing field.

Imagine if your child was empowered to tell **99** *you that sometimes you are unreasonable or that you do not always have a patent on the right solution?*

If we play on a field lacking clearly demarcated corner flags, our natural reaction is to keep the ball in play as long as possible, in order to discover how long we can do so before the referee blows the whistle. Defined corner flags are the best way to avoid highly agitated players. So, before you fly into a rage – or give your child a red card – remind yourself that your child instinctively and constantly challenges your limits with the positive intention of finding out where the line is.

The best solution is for you to be very aware of your own limits. Set them quietly, gently – and predictably, each and every time. And remember that when you have respect for your child's limits, they, in turn, will learn to respect the limits of others.

THE POSITIVE INTENTION

Conflicts have many bonuses. You have almost certainly experienced that conflicts occur between you and your child because you think your child is doing something they should not. It is worth considering that your child has a positive intention for everything they do. Once you have figured that out, you have also figured out what it is really about – and how to navigate it.

Conflicts have many bonuses. 🙿

The other day, we met a mother who desperately told us that her two year-old boy was constantly difficult, annoying and challenging during dinner. She had tried "everything possible" without it helping.

Of course, the two year-old child was challenging during dinner, as his mother tried "everything possible". There is reason to believe – although we cannot be assured – that the boy's positive intention behind his behaviour is to discover the location of the corner flags. A toddler can only discover the location of their corner flags by challenging them.

So when his mother tried "everything", he may have interpreted it as the corner flags changing location at every meal. In other words, every time he asked: "Where are my corner flags for dinner?" he got a different answer.

WHAT WILL THE CHILD ACHIEVE?

There is a simple technique for finding out the positive intentions behind our children's behaviours. With a little practice, it takes only a few seconds.

The child's age determines the choice of strategy. An older child can just be asked about their positive intention. The question may seem a little odd to them, so you can begin by helping your child to understand the issue: "When you do that, what is it you want to achieve?"

If it is a younger child, who does not yet have language, then you can do something else.

We often do
the worst
possible
thing we can
think of in
an attempt
to resolve
conflicts in
which we
ourselves are
involved.

PUT YOURSELF IN YOUR CHILD'S SHOES

We have a unique ability as humans to "put ourselves in another's shoes". We do it unconsciously when we think: "I wonder what the manager thinks about this?" But we can also, quite easily, do it consciously. You can help yourself by saying, "Now I am my little two year-old son, sitting here at the table". Next, from your child's perspective, ask, "What is this really about?" or "What is my positive intention for doing what I do during dinner?"

Behaviour which may seem incomprehensible from where we stand, and which drives us round in circles trying to interpret it, may be explained either by asking the child directly or by "asking ourselves" when we put ourselves in the child's shoes. But please be patient. It may take some time before the answer comes to you.

Similarly, conflicts centring on your child doing something which you do not like probably represent feedback that either you have been unclear in your signals or you have done something to which your child is reacting, given that our children basically like to do what we want them to do. In fact, our children will do virtually anything to live up to our expectations. Therefore, it is not necessarily your child who has to alter their behaviour. It's you!

A fundamental belief that our children do the best they can is a great help for averting emotional hijacking. How can we be mad at a child who does their best?

COMPLETE PRESENCE

"Rapport" is central to our work in supporting the developmental process in adults. It is a French term (the '-t' is silent), meaning a good and safe relationship between two or more people, where there is mutual trust and equality.

Having a good rapport is essential for *EmpowerMind Training* and coaching. If the rapport is absent from the relationship, then the very foundation for development is non-existent. Without rapport, any attempt to support the developmental process fails.

Humans are incredibly adept at creating a rapport, and we do it all the time. When you go to a cafe with a good friend, it is not long before you are both leaning across the table, talking in the same tone, being extremely attentive to each other. You trust – without reflecting on it – that you are in a confidential space. That is having a good rapport.

Rapport happens, quite naturally, when we feel good and we are in the company of people we are comfortable with.

The point is: because we know this, we can actively do something to create rapport. That is a fundamental premise learned during training as a coach or *EmpowerMind* trainer. Rapport can be established and sustained in a variety of ways. It safeguards a safe, trusting and equal relationship with others and ensures both development and mutual understanding.

PRESENCE, PRESENCE AND PRESENCE

You can also create and enjoy rapport with your child. Indeed, it is crucial for your relationship – and especially for preventing and resolving potential conflicts.

Conflict situations are often characterised by high-pitched voices, irritation, frustration, rejection and other emotional states that are the direct opposites of good rapport. We often do the worst possible thing we can think of in an attempt to resolve conflicts in which we ourselves are involved.

Parental behaviour that consciously builds a rapport enables us to reach out to our children. It is perhaps the most important prerequisite for a positive outcome to any conflict.

The following are some examples of what you can do.

Mirroring

You can "mirror" your child, so they feel more comfortable and at home in the situation. We can mirror body language, tone of voice, breathing and speech rate. We can mirror words – in the sense that we repeat some of the key words the child uses. It makes the child feel understood and acknowledged.

However, it is essential to distinguish between "mirroring" and "mimicking". The child will unconsciously perceive the mirror as positive, while they will undoubtedly experience mimicking as something negative. It takes some practice, because in the beginning it seems artificial to repeat the child's words.

Talk to the senses

Depending on which system of representation we use, we understand different "languages". Communicating with the child using their preferred system of representation is rapport-building, while the reverse breaks down rapport. You have an advantage here as you discovered your child's preferred representation system earlier (see p. 89-91).

Acknowledgement

Acknowledging your child is particularly good for building a rapport. It may sound both logical and trivial, but it is something we easily forget. You can acknowledge your child "effortlessly" by being present, listening attentively, nodding and making agreeing sounds to what they say. Remember that praise and acknowledgement are two different things (see p. 46-47).

You also acknowledge your child with thoughts, speech and body language that shows them you love them; probably the most rapport-building thing you can do.

Be congruent

When you are congruent – when there is consistency between what you think, what you say, what you show and what you do – rapport happens naturally between you.

To be provocative, in our industry, we have to put our finger on it: any and all conflicts are due to a lack of rapport. Children are actually world champions at creating rapport, but we cannot expect them to always have the energy to consciously create a rapport with parents. Therefore, we must train ourselves to be better at doing it.

HOW TO GET STARTED

If you choose to tackle the challenge of optimising your parental consciousness, then you need to be aware of the consequences.

Firstly, you will – very quickly – become uncomfortably aware of what other parents give to their children in terms of fatal and consequence-filled decisions, statements and actions, despite their best intentions!

A word of caution: parenting is one of the most sensitive areas to challenge. So, be careful not to be a smart aleck. Just think of how challenged you have been by some of what you have read in this book. We all do our best, and naturally we think that what we are doing is right for our children.

It is usually easier if we show our own vulnerability in parenting 99

A great way to share learning and knowledge with others is to share what you have done and why you have chosen that action. Other parents can then assess for themselves whether it is something they want to be inspired by. It is usually easier if we show our own vulnerability in parenting. That way we avoid being perceived as self-important or the self-proclaimed champions of parenthood.

YOUR CHILD MAY GET A CULTURE SHOCK

Your child may become confused when you change strategy. This is a natural reaction. As human beings, we (and this applies equally to the young and the old) are incredibly adept at getting accustomed to the people around us is in a certain way. Likewise, insecurity quickly results when people act differently.

Thus, if you start using the techniques in this book, you may, depending on the age of your child, encounter resistance. As we said, this is a natural instinct and does not mean that what you are doing is not working! Rather, it involves adhering to your strategy and not abandoning your effort too quickly, because one thing is certain:

If you do the same tomorrow as you did today, then there is a great probability that nothing will change.

In return, your perseverance will be rewarded with your children's acceptance of the new strategy. Our children love us more than anything on earth. They are accustomed to our quirks, and so they will accept it just like everything else we do. Once they have accepted it, then you can introduce the techniques in this book with reason, timing, awareness and feeling.

Jørgen and I have deliberately and consistently introduced this book's principles to Amelina, since she was quite young. If you start tomorrow with an older child, it is worth remembering that significant and continuous change rarely happens in one day. A complete cultural change from one day to the next will, probably, provide more resistance and frustration for all parties than it is worth.

Therefore, we recommend that, as parents, you sit down, in peace and with a good rapport built up, and discuss the following questions in detail:

♦ What in this book is the high point for you? That is, how can you, starting tomorrow, do something a little differently that will result in a rapid, positive change?

♦ What things will you then introduce, in what order and with what timescales?

♦ How will you help each other remember what you have agreed?

♦ How often will you "meet over a cup of coffee" and reflect on whether what you are doing is working as intended or if there is something that needs to be adjusted?

♦ How much attention are you willing to invest in your new style of parenting?

The *EmpowerMind* approach to our children is not a universal guide. You will soon discover where *EmpowerMind* techniques and tools are useful, and where you just have to comfort an unhappy child. Later, when the conflict has subsided – perhaps at bedtime – it may be time to talk about it, with a good rapport, complete presence and linguistic awareness on your part, thereby, creating tremendous positive change for your child and for your relationship.

It can also be a challenge for you when, shortly into the process, your child is more reflective and more independent.

Feedback from your child is a positive effect of this. They can give you feedback on how well you are doing as a parent, because their automatic resistance is replaced by an increased awareness. When one of us gets too cocky with Amelina, she responds instantly with an eye-movement that sends a very precise message that we have crossed the line – so we smile disarmingly and walk proudly away with the certainty that Amelina has retained her integrity, despite our numerous challenges to her worldview.

Trust, responsibility, ownership and influence enable people, young and old, to grow and develop. Thankfully, these steps also create more joy in everyday life, generate higher self-esteem and increase self-confidence.

What more could we wish for as parents?

DOING THE BEST WE CAN – PART II

Doing the best we can extends beyond parenting. It also applies to our children.

As parents, we have an incredibly strong core belief that our children always do their absolute best under the circumstances. This supporting core belief is a highly effective parenting tool, because it causes us to ignore the "mistakes" our children make. It can be quite difficult to get angry and scold someone who is doing their best. It is actually easier to forgive others for their almost "inexcusable" actions when we choose that core belief.

And it is precisely that core belief that we wrap ourselves in each morning, before we face the new day with its new agenda for our children. They are developing all the time, and not necessarily thinking about brushing their teeth and getting out of the door on time. There is an infinite amount of 'we-do-our-best' fabric left over to wrap ourselves in, so just take how much you need.

THE CHANGE NEEDS TO BE ANCHORED FAST

If, after reading this book, you choose to redefine your role as parents using the *EmpowerMind* techniques and tools, participating, listening and being conscious parents, then you need to be aware of the consequences for your parental identity.

It is exactly the same for managers, who choose the coaching management style. It is a journey into limbo!

It is easy enough to say, 'That's what I am going to do', but it is something else to actually do it and 'live it'.

Our behaviour is deeply connected to what we believe and, therefore, it is a prerequisite that you actually believe deep down inside that the approach we have presented in this book is the "right" one for you.

We can imagine and pretend for a good while, but if we really want to make changes – both for ourselves and for others – then the change needs to be anchored fast in our values, beliefs and beha-viour. Therein lies the key.

A SHORTCUT TO HAPPY CHILDREN

We believe that learning can be found in action. For instance, reading this book can only give insight, not learning. If you are ready to turn your new insights into real learning, then you must start, in practice, with *EmpowerMind* child involvement. Be assured that after a short time you will find that you have a shortcut to well-functioning, happy and resilient children, who have high self-esteem.

The process will, no doubt, result in you losing both control and the feeling of power over the situation. When you no longer need to manage, control, check, decide, take responsibility and comment on something, a vacuum is created, which takes some time to fill with something else. But we promise you that instead, you can delight in increased awareness and deep inner joy, knowing that you now do the best you can to give your children the best possible conditions in life.

Enjoy and have fun with the project!

To book a workshop or keynote on parental development please send a mail to: svenstrup@empowermind.dk

You are also welcome to contact us, if your have any comments or questions regarding the book.

Find EmpowerMindTraining soundfiles for you or your children at: www.empowermindshop.com

Follow me on Twitter: @jorgensvenstrup

INDEX

www.ingramcontent.com/pod-product-compliance
Lightning Source LLC
Chambersburg PA
CBHW051315120626
46547CB00015B/2245